THE SCHOOL MUSIC CONDUCTOR

Problems and Practices

in

Choral and Instrumental Conducting

By

PAUL VAN BODEGRAVEN

Chairman, Department of Music
School of Education, New York University

and

HARRY ROBERT WILSON

Chairman, Department of Music
Teachers College, Columbia University

SCHMITT, HALL & McCREARY COMPANY
MINNEAPOLIS

Discreet — prudent.
Discrete — separate.

Copyright 1942

by

HALL & McCREARY COMPANY

Printed in the United States of America

P 5373

W. Duane La Mar
421 Eldred Street
Kalamazoo, Michigan

PREFACE

This book is written particularly for use in teacher-training institutions which offer a course in conducting for majors in Music Education and also, for individual use by beginning conductors in the field. It is designed to serve as a study guide rather than as a self-sufficient, exhaustive treatise. The book is aimed specifically at the problems most frequently encountered by the conductor of high school choral and instrumental organizations but the fundamental procedures are applicable to all levels of instruction.

Most of the music work in the upper levels of our public schools culminates in group participation, the final success of which may be determined by the conductor. This is true only when the groundwork preceding such ensemble performance has been covered thoroughly. Therefore, the conductor must be concerned with the organization of the entire music department and with the kind of teaching which the individuals in his ensemble have received previously. Many competent conductors fail to achieve results because of the mistaken notion that skill in conducting is the most important requisite for success. The school music conductor is first an organizer, then a teacher, and finally a conductor. His skill as a conductor can be shown only if good organization and teaching have preceded the ensemble rehearsal. Even in the rehearsal, the school music conductor remains essentially a teacher. He must guide each individual player or singer along paths which will lead to surer control of his instrument. This growth in technical and interpretative power, brought about by correct procedures, is the goal which leads to higher and higher levels of ensemble performance. The conductor of professional ensembles may devote his entire attention to interpretation but not so the school music conductor. He must teach correct procedures of singing and playing as well as interpretation. Adequate interpretation is impossible without technical control.

In order to be a conductor, one must, of necessity, develop a baton technic. This technic, like all other musical technic, is a means to an end. It does not assure success and the conducting class in which the technic of the baton is taught exclusively is not adequately preparing the student for the job he expects to fill. Problems which pertain to conducting are best treated in a conducting class where actual demonstrations can be supplied, rather than in some methods class where the discussion is likely to become wholly academic. The sequence of problems in this book carries the student from the very first problem of baton technic to the culmination of the conductor's job, the public appearance. It is not necessary to master the chapter on baton technic before proceeding to succeeding chapters.

i

Chapters Two through Ten may be studied as the student is developing his baton technic. If the book is used properly, the student should gain a thorough knowledge of what makes for conducting success when working with school music groups.

The bibliography forms an important part of the plan of the book and some of the references at the ends of chapters should be read by the student. As was stated in the opening paragraph, this book does not pretend to be exhaustive; rather, it intends to present important subjects, to suggest a few possible solutions, and then to list reference material which can be used to study the topic more thoroughly. The problems in baton technic listed in Chapter One are those which will be encountered most frequently by the beginning conductor. If problems arise which are not covered, the reference material should be examined for possible solutions.

A feeling of hesitancy on the part of the conductor is immediately transmitted to the group under him. The only way to gain confidence is to do a lot of conducting in front of a group. This may be done at first by having the members of the class act as a chorus, singing simple songs. As each new problem is explained in Chapter One, references are made to songs which appear in *The New Blue Book of Favorite Songs* published by Hall and McCreary Company, Chicago, Illinois. Later in the course, opportunities for conducting instrumental groups and choruses singing more difficult numbers should be provided, if at all possible. The more conducting that can be done under supervision the better. *We learn to do by doing only when we are proceeding along correct lines. A person who conducts poorly may deteriorate further by practicing incorrectly.*

Finally, this book is not intended to be a self-instructor, particularly in the development of baton technic. The teacher of conducting may prefer solutions to the various problems which differ from those in the text. It should be remembered that the solutions herein presented are *a* way, not *the* way. The one rigid requirement for all solutions is that they achieve the desired results.

PAUL VAN BODEGRAVEN
HARRY ROBERT WILSON

CONTENTS

CONTENTS (Continued)

CONTENTS (Continued)

looked
over, but
didn't
read.

v

ACKNOWLEDGMENTS

Grateful acknowledgment of our indebtedness to the following publishers and authors is hereby made for permissions to quote and use the following material on which they hold copyrights: American Book Company for the quotations on page 22 from *Hollis Dann Song Series, Conductor's Book* by Hollis Dann. Belwin, Inc., for the quotations on pages 15, 26, and 73 from *Elementary Rules of Conducting* by V. Bakaleinikoff. Oliver Ditson Company, Inc., for the quotation on page 30 from *Essentials in Conducting* by K. W. Gehrkens; the quotation on page 36 from *Project Lessons in Orchestration* by A. E. Heacox; and the quotation on pages 58-59 from *Glee Club Book for Girls* by Mabelle Glenn. Carl Fischer, Inc., for the first page of the 1st Violin part of *Ballet Egyptien* by A. Luigini, arranged by Theo. Moses-Tobani, appearing on page 40; the first page of the Piano-Conductor's Score of *Jesu, Joy of Man's Desiring* by Johann Sebastian Bach, transcribed for orchestra by Charles J. Roberts, appearing on page 42; and the first page of the Full Orchestra Score of *Rosamunde Overture* by Franz Schubert, arranged by Julius S. Seredy, appearing on page 44; for the quotation on page 17 from *The Technic of the Baton* by Albert Stoessel; and the quotation on page 92 from *Band Betterment* by E. F. Goldman. Dr. Becket Gibbs for the rules for the *Italian Pronunciation of Latin* given in Appendix B. Neil A. Kjos Music Company for the Solo Cornet part of *Headliner March* by Rodney Cummings, appearing on page 46; the first page of the Condensed Score of *Mood Pastoral* by Hall M. Macklin, arranged by Russ Howland, appearing on page 47; the first page of the Full Band Score of *The Crusaders Overture* by Forrest L. Buchtel, appearing on page 48; and the quotation on page 76 from *Pitts' Voice Class Method* by Carol Pitts. Music Educators Journal for the quotations on page 58 from "High School Choral Material" by Jacob Evanson and from "What Kind of Music" by Noble Cain; the quotation on page 67 from "Essentials of Better Choral Training" by Jacob Evanson; on page 73 from "Choral Intonation" by Lyravine Votaw; on page 75 from "A Statement of Principles" by the Adolescent Voice Committee of the American Academy of Teachers of Singing; and on page 91 from "The Marching Band" by M. Hindsley. National School Band, Orchestra and Vocal Associations for permission to reprint the Adjudicator's Comment Sheets appearing on pages 68 and 69. Paul A. Schmitt Music Company and Carl Fischer, Inc., for the quotation on page 58 from *Getting Results with School Bands* by G. R. Prescott and L. W. Chidester. Silver Burdett Company for the quotations on page 110 from *The Psychology of School Music Teaching* by Mursell and Glenn. M. Witmark & Sons for the quotation on page 15 from *The Eloquent Baton* by Will Earhart. Quotations have also been made from *On Conducting* by Felix Weingartner, published by E. F. Kalmus Orchestral Scores, Inc., and Breitkopf & Haertel; *Orchestral Conducting* by A. Carse, published by Augener, Ltd.; and from *On Conducting* by Richard Wagner, published by William Reeves.

THE AUTHORS AND PUBLISHERS

CHAPTER ONE

TECHNIC OF THE BATON

The first step to be taken in learning to be a conductor is to master those fundamental motions by which the conductor makes clear his intentions to those following him. The conductor should aim to develop a technic so clear and precise that he can conduct any group without previous rehearsal, making no stops for explanations of gestures. This statement assumes that the ensemble itself has had experience in following a good conductor. The ability to follow a conductor also is a matter of training and experience. Years of usage have standardized certain fundamental gestures and it is these standardized gestures, often referred to as the technic of the baton, that we now take up.

Only hours of practice in front of a mirror, with a phonograph or radio, and in front of ensembles, will make these gestures automatic; and they must be so automatic as to need no direct attention from the conductor if he is to be free to carry out fully his many other functions.

Posture

The conductor is a leader and he should assume a positive posture. He should stand in an erect, but comfortable position with the right foot slightly in front of the left foot and with the heels slightly turned in. If the weight of the body is shifted a little forward on the balls of the feet he is more free to pivot as he conducts various sections of the ensemble. A stance with feet spread widely apart gives a very awkward appearance, especially to the audience.

The arms and hands should also assume a positive position. They should be kept in front of the body with the right hand leading. The height and degree to which the arms are extended are determined by the size of the ensemble, larger groups requiring a more extended position of the arms. Avoid the defensive position, often prevalent among song leaders, of arms extended high and wide over the head.

The Baton

The baton serves as an extension of the arm to make the conducting gestures more discernible to the ensemble. It is quite important that the beginning conductor use a very light baton so as not to tire the arm. It should be fairly long, sixteen to twenty inches, so that all arm and wrist

1

motions will be greatly enlarged. The use of a short baton will often **lead** unwittingly to the development of excessive wrist and arm action.

The baton usually is held between the thumb and the first and second fingers, the point of the contact being with the cushion below the tip of the thumb, the last joint or tip of the first finger and the middle joint of the second finger. In music with very marked rhythm the butt of the baton may be held against the palm of the hand; while in the more flowing, graceful type of music the butt will remain free so as to give more flexibility to the grip. Care should be taken to align the baton with the forearm so that it will serve as an extension of the arm as already suggested.

THE MUSIC RACK

The music rack should have a heavy base. It should be adjustable as to height and tilt of the music table. It is very convenient to have a shelf just below the table on which music, tuning bars, or other equipment may be placed. Music racks that have faulty or rusty bolts and nuts cause many disconcerting moments for conductors. There is now an excellent rack available which adjusts without the use of bolts.

There are two locations for the music rack which may be used when conducting. One location is directly in front of the conductor. When in this position the rack must be adjusted so that the lowest part of the conductor's beat will not strike it accidentally. Therefore, when glancing at the score the conductor must be looking downward continually.

The other location for the music rack is slightly to the left of the conductor so that all of the space in front of the conductor is unobstructed.

When using this location, the score is more in line with the eyes, although still slightly below their line of vision, and the left hand is readily available for turning pages; but when glancing at the score, the head must move to the left. If this location is used care must be taken not to place the rack too far to the left.

All in all, it is easy to see the justification for the remark made by Felix Weingartner: "He (the conductor) should know it (the score) so thoroughly that during the performance the score is merely a support for his memory, not a fetter on his thought."[1]

THE PODIUM

The lowest part of the conductor's beat must be clearly visible to every member of the ensemble. One of the best methods of obtaining this result is to use platforms for the ensemble, each row being raised above the row directly in front of it. This arrangement is conducive also to better musical effects but is not always feasible, especially in the case of instrumental groups or very large choral groups.

The alternative plan is to elevate the conductor. The amount of elevation required will depend on the height of the conductor himself. The very tall conductor may stand on the same level with the ensemble and still make every beat visible to each member. The shorter conductor must elevate himself enough so that when his baton is raised it can be seen clearly by all members of the ensemble as they look at their music. The bottom of the beats must remain visible. A podium which is too high makes it difficult for the participants to watch their music and see the highest part of the beat, and a podium which is too low makes it just as difficult to see the bottom part of the beat.

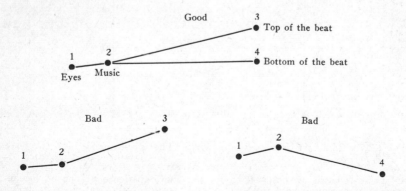

---

[1] F. Weingartner, *On Conducting*, E. F. Kalmus Orchestral Scores, Inc., 1905, p. 43.

The podium should be large enough to allow for freedom of movement on the part of the conductor, sturdy enough so that he will not worry about it breaking during a vigorous passage, and firm enough so as not to squeak when the conductor shifts his weight. It is advisable to leave an upward extension of a few inches on the side which is directly in back of the conductor so that he may not inadvertently step backwards and off the podium.[1]

THE ATTACK ON THE FIRST BEAT OF A MEASURE

The conductor is now on the podium with the music rack correctly placed and the baton properly held in his right hand. He is ready to study the problem of securing a perfect attack from the group being conducted. Let the other members of the class act as a chorus since the problem of attack is identical for all groups, choral and instrumental. Select a piece to be sung which begins on the first beat of a three-beat measure, such as "America".

The first beat of a measure always is executed by a direct down beat of the baton, but if the conductor merely beats straight down as illustrated in Example 1, he will find that the chorus has not started with him. There must be a beat, called by such various descriptive terms as the "preliminary beat", "upbeat", "preparatory beat", or "breathing beat", which precedes the first beat of the piece. This beat should move in the direction which the last beat of the measure will follow and will be executed at the exact tempo of the piece and also in the proper character. Therefore, in three-beat measure the preliminary beat will occupy the place of the third beat as illustrated in Example 2.

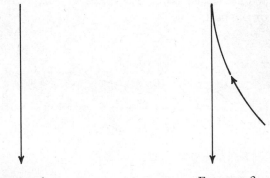

EXAMPLE 1
The first beat

EXAMPLE 2
The preliminary and first
beats for three-beat measure

---

[1] These remarks are inspired by the personal experience of one of the authors, a person of average height and weight, who has, in travels away from home with his high school groups, many times encountered all the podium difficulties enumerated.

The beginning conductor should count a measure to himself, starting his preliminary beat on the third beat in time with his counting. He might even do his counting out loud when practicing without the ensemble.

When the conductor has thoroughly grasped the characteristics of the preliminary beat and has practiced it enough to have the muscular coordination necessary to control it, he should test his ability to get an attack from the ensemble. This calls for cooperation between the conductor and the ensemble and can be perfected in no other way. If the ensemble is alert and the conductor knows his business a perfect attack will result.

The conductor may proceed step-by-step as follows:

(a) Get perfect quiet from the ensemble and then nod to the accompanist for the first chord or broken chord.

(b) Raise the baton shoulder high with the right elbow slightly bent. The wrist should not be bent. The baton should be far enough to the right of the center of the body so that when the preliminary beat is completed, the first beat will come directly in front of the body.

(c) Look at the ensemble and sense their preparedness. Both conductor and ensemble must memorize the first few notes-so that all attention can be given to securing a perfect attack.

(d) Execute the attack.

CONDUCTING THREE-BEAT MEASURE[1]

The diagram for three-beat measure is as follows:

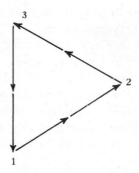

---

[1] *The New Blue Book of Favorite Songs.* Hall & McCreary Company, 1941, pp. 3, 104 (top) and 56 (bottom) are good examples since they do not represent extreme tempi or contain other unfamiliar conducting problems.

The motion for three-beat measure may be practiced to the verbal directions of *"Down, Right, Up."* As soon as the conductor beats as illustrated on page 5 he will sense that something is wrong. The beats are square and unexpressive. Actually there should be a short "rebound" at the bottom of the first beat in the direction of the following beat after which the baton executes the succeeding beats in a slightly curved manner. The actual motions now made look like this:

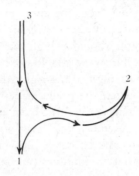

Care must be taken so as not to exaggerate this rebound to such an extent that the beat becomes undistinguishable. An excessive amount of flourish, often caused by too much wrist action, should be avoided assiduously at all times. In conducting slow legato numbers there is practically no rebound to the beat, but there seems to be continued resistance to the flow of the beat as if pulling the hand through water.

Many conductors prefer to keep the bottom of their beats as near to the center of the body as possible. In this way the conductor's face and his beat are in the direct line of vision of the ensemble. An experienced conductor uses facial expression to obtain many interpretative effects. When conducting movements are kept in front of the body and not too far to one side, the attention of the group is not divided between the facial expression and beats of the conductor.

Conducting Four-beat Measure[1]

The motion for four-beat measure is Down, Left, Right, Up, with the rebound of the first beat on the left in the direction which the second beat will assume.

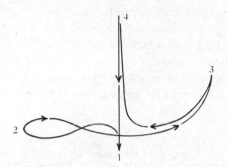

The third beat, being the secondary strong beat, is longer and more marked than the weak beats surrounding it. The preliminary beat traces the path of the fourth beat.

Conducting Two-beat Measure[2]

The motion for two-beat measure is Down, Up. The rebound of the first beat is slightly to the right, after which the second beat returns directly over the course of the first beat. The preliminary beat is up, following the direction of the second beat.

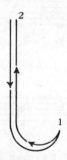

---

[1] *Blue Book* pp. 27 (top), 30 (top), 41 (bottom), 144 (bottom), 68 (bottom), **57** (top).
[2] *Blue Book* pp. 50 (bottom), 36 (bottom), 99 (bottom).

Attacks on Incomplete Measures

The conductor has learned by now, to conduct two-, three-, and four-beat measures which start on the first beat of a complete measure. A glance at any song book will show that many pieces start on incomplete measures. Here the method of obtaining a perfect attack again must be given careful consideration. The problems presented may be grouped as follows:

(a) Those met when the music starts on an incomplete measure but on a complete beat.[1] To get an attack, beat as the preliminary the beat preceding the one on which the number begins. When this causes the preliminary beat to trace the motion of a strong beat, e.g., one or three in four-beat measure, the motion should be lighter than it normally would be.

TABLE 1

Measure	Beat the piece starts on	Course of the preliminary beat
4 beat	2nd	1 (light)
4 "	3rd	2
4 "	4th	3 (light)
3 "	2nd	1
3 "	3rd	2
2 "	2nd	1 (light)

The above table shows how to use the preliminary beat to get an attack when two-, three-, or four-beat measure music starts on an incomplete measure but on a complete beat.

(b) Those problems met when the music starts on an incomplete measure and an incomplete beat.[2]

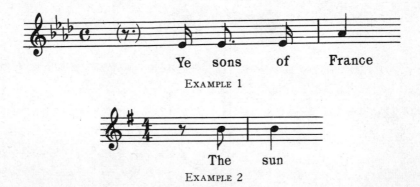

Ye   sons   of   France

EXAMPLE 1

The   sun

EXAMPLE 2

---

[1] *Blue Book* pp. 6, 7, 14 (bottom), 16 (top), 121 (bottom), 20, 24 (bottom), 39 (top), 67 (top), 164.

[2] *Blue Book* pp. 100, 26 (verse only), 237, 10 (verse only).

In these instances, the entire beat on which the music starts is given as a preliminary.

THE MOTION FOR EXAMPLE 1

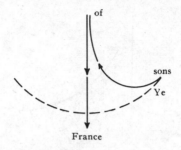

THE MOTION FOR EXAMPLE 2

On all such attacks it is imperative that both the conductor and the ensemble have a perfect conception of the sound of the beginning phrase.[1]

CONDUCTING SIX-, NINE-, AND TWELVE-BEAT MEASURES

There is quite general agreement as to the proper motions to use in conducting two-, three-, and four-beat measures, but there is no such close agreement with regard to six-, nine-, and twelve-beat measures. If we examine these measures carefully it is easy to understand how six-beat measure may be conceived as basically two-beat measure with each beat subdivided into three equal parts, nine-beat measure as being three-beat measure subdivided, and twelve-beat measure as being four-beat measure subdivided.

---

[1] For a different method of securing this attack see Gehrkens, *Essentials in Conducting*, Oliver Ditson Company, Inc., 1919. p. 30.

H. Scherchen[1] recognizes this relationship and outlines the motions for these measures accordingly, taking care that the main beats remain recognizable despite the subdivision into three equal parts.[2]

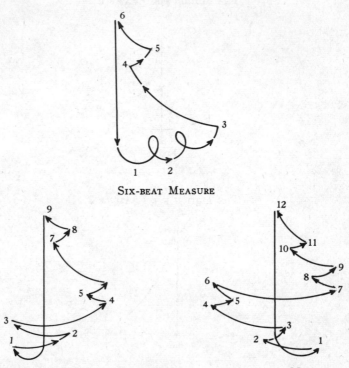

SIX-BEAT MEASURE

NINE-BEAT MEASURE   TWELVE-BEAT MEASURE

An added advantage in this method is the ease with which the beat can be changed from the subdivided beat back to the basic beat and vice versa, a change which often is convenient in a ritard or an accelerando.[3] When the tempo is too rapid to indicate each beat in six-, nine-, and twelve-beat measure, one beat is given for each unit of three so six is beaten in two, nine in three, and twelve in four.[4] Some numbers in six-, nine-, and twelve-beat meter are too fast to indicate each beat and too slow to beat only the accented beats. For such numbers a partial division of the beat is necessary. This division is indicated by beating strong accented beats and indicating the weak beat which precedes them.

---

[1] H. Scherchen, *Handbook of Conducting*, Oxford University Press, 1933, p. 156.

[2] *Blue Book*, pp. 46 (both), 67 (bottom), 183.

[3] For another method of beating six-, nine-, and twelve-beat measures see W. Earhart, *The Eloquent Baton*, M. Witmark & Sons, 1931, Chap. V, X.

[4] *Blue Book*, pp. 18, 176, 231, 180, 135.

Subdividing Two-, Three-, and Four-beat Measures

The discussion of subdivision just undertaken leads naturally to another problem which is quite similar except that the beat is to be subdivided into two equal parts. There are many times when the tempo in two-, three-, and four-beat measure moves so slowly that the baton cannot continue in a smooth, uninterrupted motion and it is found necessary to beat the second half (1 and, 2 and, etc.) of each beat.[1] Here again the form of the fundamental beat must be closely adhered to:

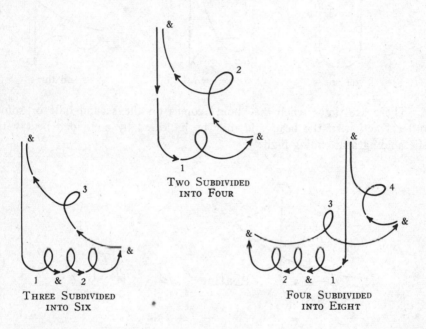

Two Subdivided
into Four

Three Subdivided
into Six

Four Subdivided
into Eight

The Hold and Release

In suggesting numbers for conducting practice up to this point it will be noticed that those which contain a "hold" (fermata) have been avoided. This problem requires special attention and hardly can be treated properly without also studying the "release", since, as the term indicates, a "hold" must be "released".

A "hold" brings about a complete stoppage, momentarily, of all rhythmic progress and, consequently, of the baton. One general principle to be observed is that the hand which indicates the "hold" (up to now, the baton hand) should be held high and should be clearly visible to all members of the ensemble.[2] This necessitates swinging off the usual course when the

[1] *Blue Book,* pp. 154, 156.
[2] *Blue Book,* pp. 42, 36, 35.

hold falls on a beat which ends in a low position such as the first, second, or third beats in four-beat measure, the motions for which are roughly:

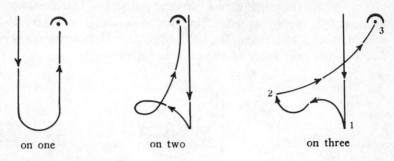

HOLDS IN FOUR-BEAT MEASURE

on one   on two   on three

There are times when the "hold" comes on the second half or some other fraction of the beat[1] and may be indicated by a divided beat with the holding beat ending high:

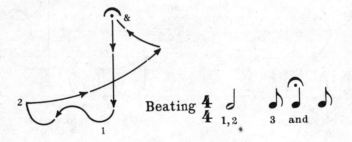

Beating $\frac{4}{4}$

Following the "hold" it is necessary, (a) to either stop the ensemble from singing or playing completely, or, (b) to have them continue without a break in tone.

(a) Stopping after a "hold" is brought about by a release beat, which is a decisive beat in a downward direction preceded by a preliminary beat.[2]

---

[1] *Blue Book*, pp. 50 (top), 49.
[2] *Blue Book*, p. 26.

When there is only a slight stoppage after the "hold", long enough to take a quick breath, the release is still downward but as much as possible in the direction which the following beat must take. The release beat may then serve as the preliminary to the following beat. This whole action then is—hold—preliminary (short)—release (preliminary for the attack) —attack.[1]

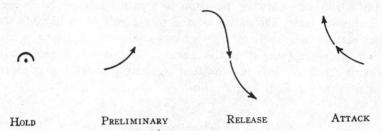

HOLD   PRELIMINARY   RELEASE   ATTACK

However, when the next attack must be made on the first beat[2] of a measure, the downward motion of the release is very short, rebounding immediately into position for the decisive down stroke.

(b) Continuing without a break after the hold is indicated by following it immediately with the next beat to be played or sung, preceded by the usual preliminary beat[3], in this order: hold—preliminary (must be short so as not to be confused with the release)—next beat.

Holds on rests usually create a problem of release and attack.[4] The release may be obtained on any beat in the measure by making the normal movment for the beat but giving it a decisive downward slant at the finish.

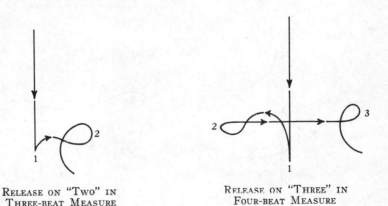

RELEASE ON "TWO" IN   RELEASE ON "THREE" IN
THREE-BEAT MEASURE   FOUR-BEAT MEASURE

[1] *Blue Book*, p. 35, third score.
[2] *Blue Book*, p. 230, (top, second score, third measure).
[3] *Blue Book*, p. 35, last score.
[4] *Blue Book*, pp. 25, 247.

Beating One in a Measure

There are many instances in which the tempo of the music is so rapid that, regardless of the measure signature, it must be conducted in one.[1] The Viennese waltzes are fine examples of this, the flowing quality of the music demanding only one beat to a bar. The motion for this beat is *down-up* with no rebound at the bottom. The conductor is conscious only of the down beat, allowing the baton to return immediately up the track of the down beat. The nature of the music will often indicate that the down beat should get the first two beats while the up stroke is made on three. There are times when the tempo is so fast that it seems advisable to divide the music into two- or four-measure phrases and conduct as if written in two- or four-beat measure.

Five- and Seven-beat Measures

Music written in five- and seven-beat measure is very rare and the young conductor is not likely to be using music of this type. There is small necessity of spending much time at the moment in thoroughly mastering this problem. The principle to grasp is that five-beat measure is a combination of two plus three or three plus two and seven-beat measure is four plus three or three plus four, each number requiring study to determine the rhythmic scheme.

Five-beat Measure

three plus two   two plus three

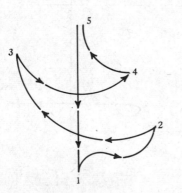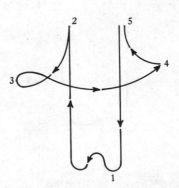

---

[1] *Blue Book*, p. 74, (bottom).

SEVEN-BEAT MEASURE

four plus three   three plus four

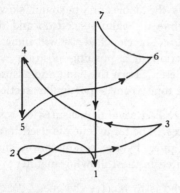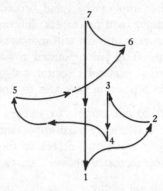

Notice that the secondary strong beat is given a downward motion although not as marked as the first beat.

THE LEFT HAND

It seems so natural to do with the left hand what the right hand is doing, that most writers on the subject of conducting state both the negative and positive functions of the left hand as is shown in the following quotations:

> "The left hand has important functions, but one point is clear; it should not become a mere additional right hand. At times, it is true, when all sections of large forces join in vigorous utterance, both hands may well pursue similar movements, may well 'beat time' alike, and thereby, almost double the animation and power of control. Usually, however, the left hand, if used at all, should perform distinct and separate duties."[1]

> "The left hand should be used only for a special occasion or purpose, for instance: an accent, a sudden piano, a sudden forte, a very important cue, etc."[2]

The three most important functions of the left hand to be mastered early are:

(a) to reinforce the movements of the right hand in situations as are described above.[3] This may take the form of a single beat or measure and rarely should be continued longer.

---

[1] W. Earhart, *The Eloquent Baton*, M. Witmark & Sons, 1931, p. 88.

[2] V. Bakaleinikoff, *Elementary Rules of Conducting*, Belwin, Inc., 1938, p. 10.

[3] *Blue Book*, pp. 150, 198.

(b) to indicate dynamics and dynamic changes, and to keep balance among sections. The hand will not beat time when indicating dynamics.

The palm of the hand turned towards the floor and the hand slowly descending will indicate a diminuendo, while the palm turned up and the arm moving upward will indicate crescendo. The clenched fist will indicate a forte. The palm pointed toward a section in a pushing position will signal that particular section only to be quieter. Turn the hand and assume a pulling position in order to draw more tone from a particular section.

(c) to cue players or singers who have had several measures of rests and to indicate the most important entrances. The term "cue" is used in all ensemble work and refers to the signal given by the conductor in such instances as stated above. It may be executed in the following manner:

1. Look at the section or individual who is to receive the cue.

2. Raise the left hand in their direction (when possible) several beats before the entrance.

3. Give the same preliminary beat before the entrance as would be given at the beginning of a composition.

4. Give the exact entrance beat and the cue is complete. Do not continue beating time for them.

Cueing is necessary especially for high school musicians but still must be used sparingly. Performers must not get so accustomed to being brought in on every occasion that they get in the habit of not counting their rest measures or of not listening to other parts to hear when their own should come in. During rehearsals, players can be trained to expect few cues except after long periods of rest or in important solo passages. This makes for alertness and listening. In a concert performance, however, the immature student needs the added confidence inspired by definite cues.

CHORAL VERSUS INSTRUMENTAL CONDUCTING

In delineating the problems of baton technic it will be noticed that no distinction has been drawn between choral and instrumental conducting technics. No such distinction need be drawn. A conducting technic which is clear and easily understandable, based on gestures which have become standardized through years of usage, need not be altered for any type of musical ensemble. The young conductor will do well to avoid "individualistic mannerisms" which are intelligible only to the group which has been trained in following them. Remember that our aim has been to develop a technic which will be understandable to any trained group at first contact.

According to Stoessel,

> "Directors of choruses must remember that essentially there is no difference between orchestral conducting and choral conducting, although there is a vast difference between orchestral and choral training and rehearsing . . . chorus members will give a rhythmical performance of a work only when they are made to feel the main pulsations of the movement, and this can only be accomplished by using such established gestures which clearly mark the fundamental rhythm."[1]

Many fine conductors, both instrumental and choral, with the latter predominating, conduct without a baton. They claim many special advantages for their way while proponents of the baton do likewise. There is considerable feeling on both sides. The most prevalent practice is to use the baton for instrumental ensembles such as the band and orchestra, and for performances by large choruses, accompanied by orchestra or piano. The baton is often dispensed with when conducting choral groups, such as a cappella choirs, glee clubs, and small mixed choruses.

No attempt will be made here to defend either viewpoint or any special practice, but mention of it must be made if the young conductor is to be well informed on his subject.* The only advice offered is to master the usage of the baton before discarding it. Conductors who can use a baton correctly are in a much better position to evaluate its utility than are those who claim preference for the batonless method, at least partially through inability to use it.

THE FUNCTION OF BATON TECHNIC

No exhaustive treatment of the subject has been attempted here. Complete books have been written demonstrating every conceivable musical problem to be met in conducting, problems which the young high school music conductor may never encounter. For this reason only the most usual problems have been discussed and general principles laid down which, if understood, will help in solving other problems.

The young conductor, learning baton technic for the first time, often feels that once these movements have been mastered he is a full-fledged conductor. Nothing is further from the truth and the writing of this

---

[1] A. Stoessel, *The Technic of the Baton*, Carl Fischer, Inc., 1920, p. 96.

* The writers have always wished, however, for a more scientific method of evaluation such as a test in which a conductor, hidden from the listeners by a screen, would conduct a group both with and without the baton while a group of competent musicians endeavored to guess when he was and was not using a baton as evidenced by the presence of a "firmer attack", "subtler nuances", and other such noticeable advantages claimed by each side.

entire book will have been a waste of time if it helps foster such an impression.

According to Carse:
> "Experience has shown that it is easier to acquire, and to teach, the purely physical part of the conductor's art than it is to cultivate those qualities which make a conductor able to rehearse and train an orchestra. The embryo conductor will—or should—face the fact that his most formidable task will be, not in learning how to manipulate the baton, but in learning to recognize faults in orchestral playing, in knowing how to eliminate them, and in gaining the power which will enable him to make the playing of the orchestra under his charge technically excellent. The physical part of conducting can be practiced alone, but the other can only be acquired by experience, and with the help of, and probably at the expense of, a real live orchestra."[1]

The possessor of an adequate baton technic is qualified to take his place on the podium and lead a group through music of any grade of difficulty, maintaining an even rhythm, indicating entrances, and suggesting dynamic markings. This is the function of baton technic. These are, however, only a few of the fundamentals of musical performance and even when they are present the final result may be extremely unsatisfactory.

The mastery of baton technic is, then, the first step to be taken in training to be a conductor, a step which anyone with a sense of rhythm can master and without which no one deserves the title of conductor.

---

[1] A. Carse, *Orchestral Conducting*, Augener, Ltd., London, 1929, p. 25.

PROBLEMS AND PROCEDURES

1. Try to recall some conductors you have played or sung under and make a list of reasons why they were easy or difficult to follow. Use these same reasons to evaluate your own baton technic.

2. Observe several conductors and discuss their baton technic in class.

3. Bring to class some problem in the technic of conducting not solved in this chapter and give your solution. See the bibliography following if help is needed.

4. Conduct, at sight, some fairly easy numbers. Do the same, allowing two minutes for study.

5. Criticize other members of the class in regard to all elements of baton technic, especially clarity, grace, and regularity of the beat.

6. Conduct and sing at the same time other songs from *The New Blue Book of Favorite Songs* than those suggested in the footnotes. Practice such conducting, both individually and as a class.

7. Conduct many numbers in the same book that have different tempi and moods. Try to make your conducting "look like the music".[1]

---

[1] To "look like the music" when conducting means larger beats when the music is *forte*, smaller beats when the music is *piano*. It means strong beats when the music is vigorous, crisp beats when it is *staccato,* and smooth flowing beats when it is *legato*. It also means indicating *crescendos* and *diminuendos* by the varied size of the beat, indicating the tapering of phrases and the inflections of words, indicating the accented beat with a beat of appropriate size, and finally, indicating rests with baton motions which retain the rhythmic flow but are in marked contrast to other beats.

SUGGESTIONS FOR FURTHER STUDY

BAKALEINIKOFF, V. *Elementary Rules of Conducting,* Belwin, Inc., 1938, Part 3.

BERLIOZ, H. *Modern Instrumentation and Orchestration,* Novello, Ewer & Co., London, 1882, p. 245, "The Orchestral Conductor".

BOULT, A. C. *The Technique of Conducting,* Hall the Printer, Ltd., Oxford, Sections 1-6.

CARSE, A. *Orchestral Conducting,* Augener, Ltd., London, 1929, Part I, Sections I-VII.

DANN, H. *Hollis Dann Song Series, Conductor's Book,* American Book Company, 1936, pp. 61-69.

EARHART, W. *The Eloquent Baton,* M. Witmark & Sons, 1931, the entire book.

GEHRKENS, K. W. *Essentials in Conducting,* Oliver Ditson Company, Inc., 1919, Chap. III.

HUBBARD, G. E. "Some Notes on Conducting," *Music Educators Journal,* Vol. XXII, (May, 1936) No. 6.

SCHERCHEN, H. *Handbook of Conducting,* Oxford University Press, London, 1933, pp. 151-188. Gives the solutions for many difficult orchestral conducting problems. An exceptionally fine book.

STOESSEL, A. *The Technic of the Baton,* Carl Fischer, Inc., 1920.

WOODS, G. H. *School Orchestras and Bands,* Oliver Ditson Company, Inc., 1920, Chap. XI.

CHAPTER TWO

FACTORS IN INTERPRETATION

No amount of musical training or sensitivity to musical expression would lead one to conduct instinctively measure signatures along the patterns heretofore described, but once these basic gestures have been mastered, the many modifications necessary to delineate the spirit, tempo, dynamics, nuances, and other niceties of musical expression should come easily and naturally, provided that the musical background of the conductor is adequate. If his musical background has been limited, it is doubtful if the conductor should attempt a job in which his musical authority must be supreme.

The most elusive elements in musical expression cannot be described with words. The conductor is here warned that he cannot become an excellent interpreter by reading books about musical interpretation; the topic is much too intangible. However, the musically mature conductor may benefit greatly by reading books such as those listed at the close of this chapter, because his musical background will lend meaning to words which otherwise would be wholly meaningless. There can be no substitute for the gift of sensitivity to the beauties of music, developed to a high degree through training in some medium of musical performance and through hearing fine music well played or sung.

Interpretation for the individual performer is an entirely personal matter. He is free to interpret the intent of the composer as he sees fit, so long as his technic is adequate to the demands he makes on it. The conductor is, however, in the position of having to make other persons feel as he does, and to see that his entire ensemble feels the same way. It is obvious, then, that the interpretative results will depend largely on the musical sensitivity of the players or singers in the ensemble since they must be able to mirror the ideas of the conductor.

There are three elements in musical expression over which the conductor exerts major control:

1. Tempo
2. Dynamics
3. Phrasing

Music which is within the technical ability of the ensemble can be.performed at the correct tempo, the dynamics can be faithfully observed, and the proper mechanical phrasing can be indicated exactly by the conductor.

Tempo

Tempo is the term used to designate the *speed* at which a musical number is performed and is the only term which should be so used. The loose usage of the word "time" results in much confusion and should be entirely eliminated.[1]

The conductor who has learned the mechanics of conducting has, at the same time, been concerned with tempo, since all beats must be indicated at a certain speed. A real problem develops, however, when a specific composition must be conducted and the proper tempo determined. This is considered by many authorities to be the most important duty of the conductor as the following two statements, one by a famous composer-conductor and the other by a famous high school music conductor will indicate:

> "The whole duty of a conductor is comprised in his ability to indicate the right tempo. His choice of tempo will show whether he understands the piece or not. With good players again the true tempo induces correct phrasing and expression, and conversely, with a conductor, the idea of appropriate phrasing and expression will induce the conception of the true tempo."[2]

> "Ability to discover and indicate the correct tempo and variations of tempo is altogether the most important duty of the conductor. It requires careful study, much experience, and musical background. There is no short cut to the attainment of this power. Even after the young conductor has decided upon the tempo, much practice in mentally singing the first phrase is often necessary before he can be at all sure that he will be able to indicate the correct tempo to the chorus. It is of greatest importance that the student of conducting learn to remember the exact tempo. Thinking and feeling the rhythmic swing of the opening of the selection over and over again is perhaps the most effective way to 'memorize' the tempo."[3]

Immature high school groups may not have perfect intonation and tone quality, but if the music being performed has been chosen in the light of the ability of the group, it will be possible to follow tempo indications closely. The entire responsibility for this rests on the conductor and he should be blamed for any errors directly relating to tempo. Indicating the correct tempo is, then, the first duty of the high school conductor but not, as Wagner suggests, for the conductor of professional groups, the entire duty.

[1] H. Dann, *Hollis Dann Song Series, Conductor's Book,* American Book Company, 1936, p. 66.
[2] R. Wagner, *On Conducting,* William Reeves, London, 1919, p. 20.
[3] H. Dann, *op. cit.,* p. 71.

The correct tempo may be determined by: (1) consulting the metro-nome marking; (2) consulting the tempo terms; (3) finding the traditional tempo; (4) using individual judgment based on the sound of the music and the spirit of the text.

METRONOME MARKINGS

Metronome markings when given, appear at the very beginning of a piece or movement. This marking indicates two things: (1) the kind of note which should be given one beat; and the number of these notes which should be played in a minute. Therefore, the marking ♩ = 60 indicates that the quarter note is the beat note and that the beat should move at the rate of 60 per minute. The newest electric metronome, the most satisfactory kind ever produced, registers tempi of from 40 to 208 beats per minute. From 40 to 60, the number intervals are spaced two apart (that is 40, 42, 44, etc.); from 60 to 72, three apart; from 72 to 120, four apart; from 120 to 144, six apart; and from 144 to 208, eight beats apart. The conductor must practice with a metronome until he can beat very close to any tempo indicated without using the metronome. In other words, he must "memorize" tempi.

The examples given below illustrate various measure signatures and the metronome marks which may accompany them. In some cases the measure signature and beat speed are the same; in others, they are different.

MEASURE SIGNATURE	METRONOME MARK	BEATS IN A MEASURE	TEMPO
2/4	♩ = 60	2	60 beats per minute
2/4	𝅗𝅥 = 60	1	" " " "
3/4	♪ = 60	6	" " " "
3/4	♩ = 60	3	" " " "
3/4	𝅗𝅥. = 60	1	" " " "
4/4	♪ = 60	8	" " " "
4/4	♩ = 60	4	" " " "
4/4	𝅗𝅥 = 60	2	" " " "
6/8	♪ = 60	6	" " " "
6/8	♩. = 60	2	" " " "
3/8	♩. = 60	1	" " " "
3/8	♪ = 60	6	" " " "

The young conductor may make some very serious mistakes if he looks only at the measure signature and then at the beat speed. When there is a metronome marking, this marking takes precedence over the measure signature although the two often agree.

Of the fours ways of determining the correct tempo, the metronome marking is mechanically by far the most exact. This can indicate only the starting speed, however, and will be of no help in making the slight variations within a movement, measure, or beat, which are so necessary in expressive playing or singing.

TEMPO TERMS

Many compositions have no metronome indication but there is instead an Italian term (or one in some other language) placed at the start which gives some indication of the tempo to be taken.

The most common of the Italian terms follow. The conductor will find many more which do not appear here but which can be found in any good music dictionary.

issimo — very

larghissimo adagissimo lentissimo grave	the very slowest tempo. Often conducted in double time with a divided beat, especially in the older classical music.
largo adagio lento	very slow tempo. Often conducted as described above.
larghetto adagietto	slow tempo. Often conducted as described above.
andante andantino	moderately slow tempo.
moderato	moderate tempo.
allegretto	moderately rapid tempo.
allegro	rapid tempo.
vivo vivace presto	very fast tempo.
presto assai prestissimo vivacissimo	most rapid tempo possible. It is often necessary and convenient to beat fewer beats than indicated in the measure signature.

There are other terms which indicate tempo fluctuations. They are used in the body of the composition rather than at the start.

più — more
meno — less

accelerando *(accel.)*
stringendo   } gradually faster
poco a poco animato

ritardando *(rit.)*   } gradually slower
rallentando *(rall.)*

piu allegro
piu presto
piu animato   } more rapid
piu mosso
un poco animato

piu lento
meno mosso } slower
ritenuto
tempo rubato—a flexible tempo
tempo giusto—a very exact tempo
a tempo—return to the regular tempo. Usually used after
    an accelerando or ritardando to indicate a return
    to the previous speed.
tempo I (tempo primo)—return to the first tempo
alla marcia—march time
tempo di valse—waltz tempo

ad libitum   } at the pleasure of the performer—
a piacere   } no exact tempo.

In connection with the interpretation of the above tempo indications the conductor must be aware of certain standard practices. The introductions of the older classical works with tempo markings of *adagio, molto adagio,* or *largo,* require the beat to be doubled so that two-beat measure contains four beats, three-beat measure contains six beats, and so on.[1] When this is done the tempo of the doubled beat must not be too slow since doubling the beat reduces the tempo by one-half. Compositions which have a marking of *allegro,* or *presto,* or other rapid tempo indications, are often written in *alla breve* (¢) measure. This automatically doubles the speed and so care should be taken not to beat *alla breve* too rapidly.[2]

Compositions marked *Tempo di Valse* will bear a 3/4 measure signature but are usually conducted with one beat to the measure, particularly if they are written by composers such as Johann Strauss or Waldteufel.

[1] The opening of the Haydn D Major (London) Symphony is a good example.
[2] The fourth movement of the Mozart Jupiter Symphony is a good example.

It must be thoroughly understood that the Italian terms indicate a very general tempo, not a specific one. It is not possible to say that *andante* varies on the metronome from 72 to 84. If the student will notice the Italian terms in some classical music then listen to a recording of the number and time the rate of speed with a metronome, he will find that *andante* may have a faster metronome indication than *allegro*. Therefore, a great deal of individual judgment is necessary in finally determining the tempo, even when Italian tempo terms are given.

TRADITIONAL TEMPO

Every piece of music which has been played for any length of time has a tempo which has been determined by tradition. Only the person who has heard these numbers played over and over by fine ensembles can be counted on to conduct the number in the correct tempo. Learning such tempi exclusively by listening to records is a dangerous method, although at times the only feasible one. Some recordings have incorrect tempi, not because the conductor is unaware of them, but because the music must be speeded up or slowed down to fit on the record. Moreover, when this method is used care must be taken that the phonograph is set at the proper speed.

In addition to problems of initial tempi, there are other problems such as those indicated by the following statement:

> "Some of these universal musical traditions are that the ending of every Minuet in the classic works, and the last few chords of every Finale are played with a slight ritard; and a Fugue, if it is in the middle of a movement, is played a little bit slower than the rest of the movement. The student will never fail if he will follow the universal traditions, but other traditions, which many conductors do differently with certain compositions, are always disputable, and the student should be very careful about adopting them."[1]

TEMPO DETERMINED BY JUDGMENT

There are many times when the conductor must rely entirely on his own judgment in determining the tempo. He must play or sing over the music, study its rhythmic scheme, read the text in vocal music, and then select the speed which "feels" right. Needless to say, this requires a fine musical background plus careful study. Some composers use no tempo

---

[1] V. Bakaleinikoff, *Elementary Rules of Conducting*, Belwin, Inc., 1938, p. 24.

indications whatsoever because they have found that conductors disregard them anyway and because they feel the conductor should be a thorough enough musician to determine the correct tempo unaided by metronome indications or musical terms.

> "Sebastian Bach, as a rule, does not indicate tempo at all, which in a truly musical sense is perhaps best. He may have said to himself: whoever does not understand my themes and figures, and does not feel the character and expression, will not be much the wiser for an Italian indication of tempo."[1]

Another remark by Wagner is quite significant for the non-singing instrumentalist:

> "The right comprehension of the Melos (melody in all its aspects) is the sole guide to the right tempo; these two things are inseparable; the one implies and qualifies the other.
>
> ". . . . . our conductors so frequently fail to find the true tempo because they are ignorant of singing."[2]

It is not possible to develop musical judgment by reading about it. Therefore, the only thing possible here is to call the student's attention again to the necessity of having a fine musical background if he wishes to succeed as a conductor.

DYNAMICS

To those with a fine background of musical experience, dynamic marks, i.e., the comparative loudness and softness of tones, will present no great problem. The one danger is that heretofore the student may have relied upon his teacher to decipher any but the most common markings while now, as a conductor, he becomes the teacher and must assume this added responsibility. The most common Italian terms referring to dynamics are given here but the student also is advised to provide himself with a handbook on musical terms which will give him the meanings of less common terms as needed.[3]

TERMS REFERRING TO ONE DEGREE OF POWER

pianissimo *(pp)* — very softly
piano *(p)* — softly
mezzo (half) piano *(mp)* — medium softly
mezzo forte *(mf)* — medium loudly
forte *(f)* — loudly
fortissimo *(ff)* — very loudly

---

[1] R. Wagner, *On Conducting*, William Reeves, London, 1919, p. 20.
[2] *Ibid.* pp. 18, 19.
[3] T. Baker, *Dictionary of Musical Terms*, G. Schirmer, Inc., or W. D. Clark, *An Illustrated Dictionary of Modern Musical Instruments*, Hall & McCreary Company, 1928.

The usual way to indicate such marks of expression is to use a long beat far from the body for *ff* and a short beat close to the body for *pp*. The palm and fist of the left hand will come into use only at the start of each new dynamic change or as a warning to sections that they are not satisfactorily executing the dynamic markings.

TERMS REFERRING TO FLUCTUATIONS IN POWER

piu piano — more softly
piu forte — more loudly
forte-piano *(fp)* — loudly, followed *at once* by softly. Indicate *fp* by a vigorous, rapid beat, with a correspondingly longer time spent at the end of the beat, followed by a short beat.

sforzando ⎫*(sfz)* — accent or stress the note or chord so marked.
sforzato   ⎭   Execute like the *fp* except that the following beat may be *p*.

crescendo *(cresc.)* — gradually becoming louder. Increase the length of the beat.

diminuendo *(dim.)*   ⎫—gradually becoming softer. Decrease the
decrescendo *(decresc.)*⎭ length of the beat.

crescendo poco a poco — becoming louder little by little

crescendo subito — becoming louder suddenly

crescendo e diminuendo *(cresc. e dim.)* — gradually louder, then gradually softer

Crescendos and diminuendos should be gradual and even, unless some abrupt effect is indicated in the music. The following diagrams give visual representation of correct and faulty crescendos and diminuendos.

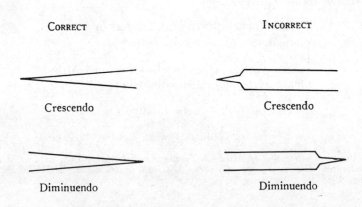

CORRECT   INCORRECT

Crescendo   Crescendo

Diminuendo   Diminuendo

It is extremely important to understand that dynamic markings are relative in their meaning. Forte means loudly, but what is loudly? For the mature performer or ensemble it means one gradation of tone; for the immature ensemble it means another. An accent coming in a pianissimo passage means an entirely different thing than it does when appearing in a forte passage. A crescendo from an *f* to *ff* sounds far different than does a crescendo from *pp* to *p*. The conception of an *fp* held by a placid type of high school performer will vary greatly from that conceived by his conductor unless he is also a placid type. One's conception of crescendo and diminuendo may be entirely changed by hearing such a number as Ravel's Bolero played by a fine orchestra under a fine conductor, for this number is one long crescendo followed by a long diminuendo. Such are the experiences which finally produce sound musicianship.

The dynamic markings in ensemble music are rarely exact. The usual thing to do is mark *p* straight down the score when, as a matter of fact, one part may actually need to be played *pp* or *mf* in order to maintain the musical sense of the composition. Melody parts must be slightly louder than the supporting parts and must, therefore, be played louder, or the other parts must be played softer; however, these levels of dynamics are seldom indicated in the score. Experienced orchestral players on solo instruments such as the oboe, clarinet, or flute, usually play solo passages one degree louder than marked. A choir in which the men's voices are far more powerful than the women's voices must understand that *ff* is a very relative term, the execution of which will always be governed by good taste as evidenced by balance and blend.

The following points should be given consideration in the execution of dynamics:

① In a crescendo, two problems must be considered: how long is it to last, and how far will it be carried. The same problems occur when executing a diminuendo.

② When no dynamic change is indicated the tone-gradation must be kept at one level. A forte which lasts for several measures must not deteriorate into a mezzo-forte. A pianissimo must not develop into a piano.

③ When an explosive effect or sudden change is indicated the change must be as rapid and great as it is possible to make it. In executing a *fp* there is often a tendency to sustain the forte too long and then drop to mezzo-forte instead of to piano. Such an effect requires excellent control of the tone.

PHRASING

Music is made up of short sections, called phrases, of varying length which are somewhat complete in themselves but combine to make an intelligible whole.   Phrases in music may be compared to phrases in a literary composition. When reading such a composition the rise and fall of the voice will indicate the punctuation marks which divide a sentence into component parts.   In this way the meaning of the entire sentence is made clear and a mistake in the placement of one comma may change the meaning of the entire sentence.   Phrases in music must be similarly separated. The conductor has almost complete control in this mechanical part of phrasing since he can indicate the proper ending of phrases by a slight cessation of the beat, just enough to indicate a breathing place, without actually holding up the continuous flow of the music. The finer art of phrasing, the treatment of each note within the phrase in the light of its importance, is another matter, and specific directions for its accomplishment cannot be successfully undertaken in a book of this kind.

The phrases in vocal music can be recognized easily by a close study of the text. The words should be read aloud several times until the conductor is certain of the meaning which the composer wishes to convey, then slight pauses should be made which will make this meaning clear. The general rule for phrasing in choral music is to follow the text, but occasionally the rule may be broken to bring out the surge of a musical phrase. The common mistakes in phrasing made by choral groups, as given by Gehrkens, are all directly traceable to an ignorance of the real meaning of the text:

1. Taking breath unnecessarily in the middle of a phrase.
2. Breathing between syllables of a word.
3. Dividing a long phrase improperly.
4. Running over breathing places when a pause is really necessary in order to bring out the meaning of the text.
5. Pronouncing the unaccented syllable of a word at the end of a phrase with too much stress.
6. Failing to stress the climax sufficiently."[1]

The band and orchestra conductor must depend entirely upon his musical judgment to discover the proper endings of phrases. Once these have been decided upon, markings should be placed in each part, indicating where breath should be taken or slight pauses made. If the conductor leaves this to the judgment of his immature players, then he does not retain the control over the mechanical part of phrasing heretofore claimed for him. It is significant that conductors of many fine symphony orchestras take the time to go over every single part to see that all phrases are marked as well as to check all dynamic marks, bowing, etc. If such painstaking care is necessary in conducting fine professional groups, the school conductor would hardly be justified in doing less.

---

[1] K. W. Gehrkens, *Essentials in Conducting,* Oliver Ditson Company, Inc., 1919, p. 68.

Problems and Procedures

1. Find a piece of music which has no tempo indication. Compare your choice of tempo with that of other conductors. Check the tempi with a metronome so as to record the exact variance between them.

2. Set the metronome at any speed and guess the tempo being heard, giving the exact numerical speed such as, 84, 72, etc. Check your answer carefully for exactness in tempo and in the use of markings found on the metronome.

3. Designate various metronome markings and then beat the correct tempo. Count aloud and set the metronome in motion at the tempo given in order to show up agreement or disagreement.

4. Write the first sentence of *America* with correct punctuation marks. Do the same for other songs you know. Now compare your work with a correct copy. Did your version show a complete understanding of the meaning of the text?

5. Find some songs containing word phrases which do not seem to agree with the musical phrases. Study the phrasing of these songs.

6. Practice conducting many chorales, making a special study of *(fermata.)*

7. Practice conducting numbers which have a quick change of tempo or dynamics. Be careful to adjust your conducting beat immediately wherever the changes occur. *Make your conducting "look like the music".*[1]

---

[1] See footnote, p. 19.

Suggestions for Further Study

CAIN, N. *Choral Music and Its Practice*, M. Witmark & Sons, 1932, Chap. XII.

COWARD, H. *Choral Technique and Interpretation*, Novello & Co., Ltd., London.

EARHART, W. *The Eloquent Baton*, M. Witmark & Sons, 1931, Chap. VI, VII.

FINN, W. J. *The Art of the Choral Conductor*, C. C. Birchard & Company, 1939, Chap. I and XII.

GEHRKENS, K. W. *Essentials in Conducting*, Oliver Ditson Company, Inc., 1919, Chap. IV-VII.

GREENE, H. P. *Interpretation in Song*, The Macmillan Company, Ltd., London, 1931, Chap. VI, VII.

STOESSEL, A. *The Technic of the Baton*, Carl Fischer, Inc., 1920, Chap. V.

WAGNER, R: *On Conducting*, William Reeves, London, 1919.

WEINGARTNER, F. *On Conducting*, E. F. Kalmus Orchestra Scores, Inc., 1905.

CHAPTER THREE

SCORE READING

Many high school students become very proficient in the correct use of the baton, being able to lead a group through quite intricate numbers. When, however, they are confronted with a full orchestral or band score, many of them are unable to use it to advantage. It is at this point that the well prepared teacher begins to show the superiority of his knowledge over that of his students because score reading is a specialized ability which is acquired only through practice.

Learning to use a score efficiently is a great deal like learning to sight-read fluently. Professional musicians can perform astounding feats of reading, but this ability is not heaven-sent. It is the result of hours and years of practice in reading. The ability to read scores is likewise the result of hours of practice and study. Just as our players progress from simple tunes to more difficult ones, so must the conductor develop his ability.

Many of our school conductors are unable to use a full score, and are so unwilling to learn that publishers rarely think it necessary to print a full score when publishing a number meant primarily for school use. When they do so, it often turns out to be a losing venture as witness the experience of one publisher who sold 650 copies of a band number but only 75 full scores. Five hundred seventy-five conductors chose to use a condensed score even when a full score was available. There has been an encouraging increase in the number of full band and orchestra scores available for school numbers within the past few years, a trend which may be expected to continue if conductors use full scores and refuse to use numbers for which they are not provided. In the meantime, the young conductor is confronted with the necessity of learning to use a conglomerate mixture of incomplete, half-complete, and complete conductor's parts and to teach his groups thoroughly in spite of such handicaps. *Music teachers should use a full score whenever it is available. In light of greater teaching efficiency full scores are more economical than incomplete scores.*

CHORAL SCORES

The student who has studied Chapter One, using the suggested songs, already has had experience in reading one kind of vocal score. Songs were used to illustrate the different technical problems of baton technic because they represent the easiest type of score to read. The most common vocal scores which the young high school teacher will be called on to read are

33

those for two- and three-part female voices, two-, three-, and four-part male voices, and two-, three-, and four-part mixed chorus. The following four-part mixed chorus score from *Goodnight* will illustrate the few problems which demand attention:

Goodnight
Chorus for Mixed Voices, A Cappella
(S.A.T.B.)

SELMA E. MARKOWITZ   HARRY ROBERT WILSON

This lovely poem is in the style of a villanelle and there is lasting beauty in these old forms. The composer has closely followed the mood and formal structure of the poem. The contrasting middle-section in a related key soars to a splendid climax as the chords seem to melt smoothly together before returning to a quiet close.

All tenor parts written in treble clef are sung an octave lower than indicated in the score. In order to be absolutely correct in the writing of tenor parts, which when written in the bass clef entail the use of many ledger lines, some composers use the following clef signs:

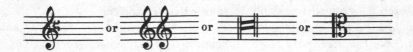

or some variant of these signs which indicate that middle C is represented by the line or space where the two short lines join the main vertical line. When being used for the tenor voice, middle C is placed on the third space and can be read exactly like the treble clef but sounds an octave lower.

The placing of each voice on a separate staff sometimes causes difficulty when the voice parts must be played, especially when the accompaniment does not contain each voice part. A little practice in reading these open scores will soon make them easier to read but, if in the meantime, a rehearsal must be conducted from such a score, the conductor may re-write the number in the style used in hymn books and song collections. The condensation provided for the first brace of *Goodnight* looks like this:

Most choral octavo editions of a cappella arrangements provide such a condensation of voice parts to be used in rehearsal.

When inexperienced student accompanists must be used, it will be especially helpful to use the above procedure. *However, all accompanists should practice reading open choral scores, in order that they may have more facility during part rehearsals.*

TRANSPOSITION

Before the more complicated tasks of reading band and orchestra scores can be taken up, the student must be introduced to one of the most provocative problems of music notation, that of the use of transposing instruments. Rarely is this problem presented to a music student for the first time without his immediately offering many suggestions for a revision of the practice. The reasons for using transposing instruments are not as important to us here as is the fact that they are used and will probably continue to be used for many more years, so the conductor will be wise to first understand the present usage before spending much time and energy in mapping out simplifications.

There are many so-called short cuts and simplified methods of mastering the problem of transposition. There are also many convenient "Charts" which will reveal immediately in what key the cornet is playing when the violin is playing in the key of A, etc. Sooner or later all these makeshift methods lead into difficulties and, after much wasted effort, the conductor must finally conclude that the only safe way to solve the problem of transposition is to understand the basic principles on which it works, and then practice solving problems in transposition until it is no longer a problem for him.

A transposing instrument is one which *plays* one note but *sounds* a pitch higher or lower than the one played. Heacox describes the procedure as follows:

> "For purposes of illustration, suppose that at the end of a long vacation, you return to find that your piano has gone below pitch; so much so that when you strike middle C, you get B♭, a whole step lower. You play a song written in C, it sounds as if written in B♭. Your piano has become a transposing instrument. It is in B♭. Because of this, if you really want your song to sound in C, you must play it a whole step higher than that—that is the key of D. To avoid the difficulty of reading from a copy in C and transposing it up a whole step, as you go, you will prefer a copy printed in D which can be played as written and your piano (now in B♭) will do the transposing itself."[1]

The first principle of transposition then is that the written notation and the actual pitch sounded, differ by varying degrees. The conductor must first be able to tell what actual pitch is indicated by notation written for a transposing instrument. In order to do this it must be made clear which instruments transpose and which do not. The instruments usually found in school organizations and their classifications are as follows:

NON-TRANSPOSING INSTRUMENTS

Strings	Wood-winds	Brasses
violin	C flute	trombone—bass clef
viola	oboe	baritone—bass clef
cello	bassoon	tuba

TRANSPOSING INSTRUMENTS

Strings	Wood-winds	Brasses
string bass	D♭ flute and piccolo	all cornets
	all clarinets	all horns
	all saxophones	trombone—treble clef
	English horn	baritone—treble clef

With one exception, all instruments which play in the bass clef are non-transposing. The string bass is the exception but the transposition

---

[1] A. E. Heacox, *Project Lessons in Orchestration,* Oliver Ditson Company, Inc., 1928, p. 79.

is very simple, the pitch sounded being an octave below the note played, i.e.,

PLAYS—SOUNDS

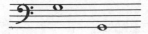

The pitch names of all instruments should be memorized since this is an important cue in solving the transposition. All instruments playing in treble clef and pitched in C such as the C flute and oboe, are nontransposing. An instrument is named from the actual pitch sounded when C is played. The cornet becomes a B♭ cornet because, when C is played, the actual pitch sounded is B♭. The problem then is to determine whether the pitch sounded is above or below the C being played.

The following chart of instruments reading in the treble clef shows this clearly and must be thoroughly memorized. The instruments which, when playing C, produce a higher pitch are above the heavy line and those which produce a lower pitch are below the line. It will be noticed that only three instruments sound higher pitches, and two of these, the D♭ flute and the E♭ clarinet, are not commonly used.

INSTRUMENT	INTERVAL SOUNDED BELOW OR ABOVE MIDDLE C	ACTUAL PITCH SOUNDED
D♭ Piccolo	Octave and a minor second	D♭
E♭ Clarinet	minor third	E♭
D♭ Flute	minor second	D♭
B♭ Clarinet, cornet, trumpet, soprano saxophone	major second	B♭
A Cornet, clarinet	minor third	A
F Horn, English horn	perfect fifth	F
E♭ Horn, alto clarinet, alto saxophone	major sixth	E♭
B♭ Tenor saxophone, trombone, baritone, bass clarinet	Octave and a major second	B♭
E♭ Baritone saxophone	Octave and a major sixth	E♭

C

To further illustrate how transposition works, the whole notes in the following examples indicate the note played and the filled in note, the pitch sounded: Example (a) in each case shows the pitch sounded when C is played. Examples (b) and (c) show the pitches sounded when certain other tones are played.

The pitch names of the common non-transposing instruments reading in bass clef are:

     B♭ baritone, trombone
     E♭ tuba
     BB♭ tuba (usually called the double B)

A great deal of confusion often results when the conductor asks a player of a transposing instrument to play a given note. When the conductor tells a B♭ cornet player to play B♭ he will do as he is told and the resultant pitch will be A♭. If the conductor had wanted the player to actually sound B♭ he should have said, "play *concert* B♭." When referring to the actual pitch to be sounded always preface the pitch with the adjective "concert," as "concert C, A, F." Very young players will not understand the problem involved and the conductor must name the note to be played. Therefore, if the conductor wants the pitch of B♭ to be sounded, he must direct the B♭ cornets to play C, the F horns F, the D♭ piccolo A, etc.

This leads us to another problem which is merely an inversion of the one already solved and is illustrated in the last two sentences of the statement by Heacox. We have dealt with the problem of determining the actual pitch sounded when a transposing instrument is playing a part written for that particular instrument. In almost all cases the actual pitch sounded was found to be below the note written in the part; which means that it was necessary to write the part to be played above the actual pitches desired. A B♭ cornet sounds a pitch a major second *below* the note indicated in the score, therefore, the part must be written a major second *above* the pitch to be sounded. In giving directions it is necessary to name the note which, when played, will yield the actual pitch desired. The chart previously given can now be used by referring to the intervals sounded below or above the note played. The instruments which *sound* a major second below the note played, must be told to play a major second *above* the pitch desired. The F horn must play a perfect fifth *above,* the D♭ piccolo an octave and a minor second *below,* etc. In order to obtain concert B♭, the tuning note for the band, the B♭ cornet must play C, the F horn F, the piccolo A.

The problem of transposition is often quite confusing to the young conductor at first but until a ready facility is developed in (1) naming the actual pitch indicated by a part written for a transposing instrument, and (2) naming the note which a transposing instrument must play in order to get a specified concert pitch, the actual problem of reading the score and understanding it can hardly be undertaken with full success.

ORCHESTRAL SCORES

Since the published editions of orchestral compositions vary, the high school orchestral conductor must learn to lead his group reading from a first violin part, a piano-conductor part, or a full-score. These parts and scores will be treated in the order named.

The First Violin Part

The first violin part shown on the next page is very easy to read and, so far as the reading goes, involves few problems. The problem created by it is the lack of any definite knowledge of what the other members of the orchestra are supposed to be doing. The only way to obtain this knowledge is to study every part separately and then remember the most important features of each part, possibly indicating such parts by adding

A First Violin Part to be Used by the Conductor

"Ballet Egyptien"

1ST Violin.

Small Orch. $2.00 | Full Orch. $3.00
Grand Orch. $3.75 | Piano Acc. .50¢
Extra String Parts .30¢ each. | Wind Parts .25¢ each.

NO I.

Revised Edition.
A. LUIGINI.
arr. by Theo. Moses-Tobani.

Theatre Orch. Allegro non troppo. (♩ = 108)

753.

7472–103

Printed in the U.S.A.

notes in the first violin part. Weingartner expressed his opinion of conducting from the first violin part as follows:

> ". . . Habeneck of Paris, as Berling tells us, conducted not from the score but from a violin part, a custom today confined to beer-garden concerts with their waltzes and potpourries."[1]

When the first violin part is the only conducting score available it indicates what instrument is playing the melody. When it is in the first violin, it does not indicate what other instruments are also playing it. When the melody is not in the first violin an extra staff is often added above the violin part showing the *concert* pitches of the melody and indicating what instrument is playing it. When such a melody is being played by a transposing instrument, the conductor must make the necessary adjustments between the written notes and the concert pitches. When the first violin has nothing to play, there are often small cued notes written around the rests to indicate to some degree what is going on in other sections of the orchestra.

We may conclude, therefore, that while the first violin part is easy to read, it is very difficult to conduct from and should never be used when a more complete score is available. When it must be used, all orchestral parts must be studied before the rehearsal and a memorandum made of their most important features.[2] There may be times when the conductor finds it advisable to make a full score for himself[3], but because of the tremendous amount of time required, this can hardly be urged on the young conductor as a common practice to be followed with all numbers.

The Piano-Conductor Score

The Piano-Conductor part is of more value to the conductor than is the first violin part because it shows the harmony as well as the melody and gives a more complete idea of everything that is going on in all parts of the orchestra. It goes without saying that it is still far from satisfactory as a real guide for the conductor. The notation gives concert pitches and the conductor must make the necessary changes when speaking to players of transposing instruments.

As when using the first violin part, all parts included in the orchestration must be studied separately and notations of important features added to the Piano-Conductor part.

[1] F. Weingartner, *On Conducting*, E. F. Kalmus Orchestra Scores, Inc., p. 7.
[2] Glenn H. Woods, *School Orchestras and Bands,* Oliver Ditson Company, Inc., Chap. XVI, "How to Make a Conductor's Part".
[3] *Ibid.,* Chap. XIV, "How to Assemble an Orchestra Score".

A PIANO-CONDUCTOR SCORE

Jesu, Joy of Man's Desiring
from "Cantata No. 147"
(Choral Melody by Johann Schop)

Piano Acc.
(Conductor)

Small Orch. $1.05   Full Orch. $1.50
Grand Orch. $2.00

JOHANN SEBASTIAN BACH
Transcribed for Orchestra
by Charles J. Roberts

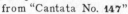

T 2126

*Original tempo indicated as ♩ = 80.

28434-29

The Full Score

Now we come to the full score itself, the only score which is really satisfactory in all respects. It is difficult to follow at first, but it gives the conductor a complete picture of what to expect from every instrument in the orchestra so that the actual job of rehearsing is greatly simplified. It is unfortunate that so few full scores are available for the easier numbers played by immature high school groups, because the less capable the player the more help he will need from the conductor. The conductor is in no position to offer such help when he does not know exactly what is expected through lack of a full-score.

Examination of a few full orchestral scores will show that all are made according to the same plan. The wood-wind family is on top, followed by the horns, then the brass family, the percussion, the strings, and finally, the piano part which is only rarely supplied. The instruments in each family are listed according to pitch from high to low. When each family of instruments is not indicated by brackets, it is helpful to bracket them as follows:

{ flute
  oboe
  clarinet
  bassoon

{ horns
  trumpets
  trombones
  tuba

  percussion

{ 1st violin
  2nd violin
  viola
  'cello
  bass

The student must memorize the order in which the families of instruments are listed and also the place given to each instrument within its family.

The viola plays in alto clef ⬚ which places middle C on the third line.

The tenor clef ⬚ places middle C on the fourth line. It is used in the 'cello, trombone, and bassoon parts when the pitches run so high as to necessitate the use of many ledger lines in the bass clef.

THE FULL ORCHESTRA SCORE

Rosamunde
(Die Zauberharfe — The Magic Harp)
OVERTURE

FRANZ SCHUBERT, Op. 26
arr. by Julius S. Seredy

When first using a full score, the young conductor may find it necessary to concentrate on a single staff such as the first violin in order not to lose the place. Needless to say, so long as this is necessary the full score will be more of a liability than a help. Ability should be developed to the point where the important features of an entire page can be seen at a glance and the staff assigned to any instrument located immediately.

Miniature scores will often list all of the instruments to be used in a movement of a symphony on the first page and then reduce the staves on the following pages to the actual number needed for the instruments having parts to play on those pages. This practice saves space but can result in a great deal of confusion if the conductor is not alert.

Appendix A contains a list of orchestral terms which will be very useful when reading foreign publications of orchestral scores.

A complete understanding of the different types of bowing on stringed instruments is necessary in order to teach properly the inexperienced player. This understanding is best obtained through actual practice or close observation of experienced string players.

BAND SCORES

Published editions of band numbers supply the conductor with a solo cornet part, a condensed score, or a full score.

The Solo Cornet Part

For years the solo cornet part was the only part published for the conductor, and he will still find that many numbers he wishes to play have no other conductor's part. As with the first violin part, this part is easy to read but difficult to conduct from. This practice is a hold-over from the military brass band in which the cornet almost always carried the lead and the conductor often played the solo cornet part as well as directing from it.

The solo cornet part shows where the melody is, cues in some of the important baritone, trombone and bass counter-melodies, and gives an occasional important bass drum beat or cymbal crash. A great deal is condensed on a single staff but much more is omitted than is shown. All parts shown are in the Bb cornet key and therefore represent pitches sounding a major second lower than concert pitches. When giving directions to players of non-transposing instruments this must be taken into consideration.

THE SOLO CORNET PART

1st Bb Cornet (Solo)
(Conductor)

HEADLINER
March

RODNEY CUMMINGS

Used by permission of the copyright owner, Neil A. Kjos Music Company, Chicago.

The Condensed Score

There are several varieties of condensed scores being published, all of which are more satisfactory than the solo cornet part, and none of which will satisfy the demands of the conscientious conductor who wants as complete information about his ensemble as is given the conductor of a symphony orchestra.

Most condensed scores are written on two, three, or four staves and indicate harmonies as well as melodies. The lead parts are well indicated but this is not true of the lower parts where players need the most help. The conductor will find it necessary to study all parts separately and then make notations about them in the condensed score. Condensed scores are all written in concert pitch and necessary changes in transposition must be made when speaking to players of transposing instruments.

THE CONDENSED SCORE

2

MOOD PASTORAL

Conductor

By HALL M. MACKLIN
Arr. by Russ Howland

Ed. No. 40B
International Copyright Secured

Copyright 1941 by Neil A. Kjos Music Co. Chicago, Ill.
Printed in U.S.A.

All Rights Reserved

The Crusaders
OVERTURE

FORREST L. BUCHTEL   1

Used by permission of the copyright owner, Neil A. Kjos Music Company, Chicago.

The Full Score

Full scores for band music, especially the easier numbers, are still too
infrequently published. This is unfortunate because it is the only type
of score from which the conductor may teach intelligently.

The student who has learned to read the full orchestral score will
have no trouble with the full band score. The band score has not been
standardized but the families of instruments are often listed in the following order:

> wood-winds
> saxophones
> brasses
> percussion

The placing within the families is not strictly according to pitch:

Wood-wind Order

Piccolo, flute, oboes, English horn, bassoon, E♭ clarinet,
B♭ clarinet, alto clarinet, bass clarinet.

Saxophone Order

Soprano, E♭ alto, tenor, baritone, bass.

Brass Order

Cornets, trumpets, horns, trombones, baritone, tubas, (String bass)

Percussion Order

Snare drum and triangle, bass drum and cymbals, tympani.

It is some help to the eye to bracket each family of instruments plainly
if the score is not printed in such a manner.

PRACTICING SCORE READING

Learning to read a full score readily requires several years of systematic
practice. It is advisable to start on scores which contain only a few parts
and then gradually add more complicated ones. Bakaleinikoff[1] suggests
starting with string trios, then proceeding to string quartets, then string
quartets or quintets with one transposing instrument like the B♭ clarinet,
then string sextets or septets with additional transposing instruments, and
finally to small orchestra scores such as those of Mozart, Haydn, and the
first period Beethoven. Another authority[2] begins with the simple choral
scores and gradually works into the smaller scores using transposing
instruments.

[1] V. Bakaleinikoff, *Elementary Rules of Conducting,* Belwin, Inc., 1938, p. 16.
[2] M. Bernstein, *Score Reading,* M. Witmark & Sons, 1932.

The ensemble literature for string and wind instruments has been greatly expanded in recent years and the scores of such ensembles, using, as they do, small groups of transposing instruments, makes very valuable practice material. If no small ensemble material is available for practice the student may start in at once reading from the full score but concentrating his entire attention on reading only one family of instruments at a time, preferably beginning with the string family.

For full-score reading, the miniature score is the most practical because of the cost.[1] It is extremely valuable to practice score reading at the piano as well as away from the piano. The conductor will discover many things at the piano which he will not see during a silent reading.

Preparing a Score for Rehearsal

The young conductor should never attempt to conduct a rehearsal from full score until he has studied the score so thoroughly that its essential details are memorized. As an aid to the eye which must cover so much at a glance, many conductors use colored pencils to mark important entrances, melodies, counter-melodies, and particularly important dynamic markings. A red pencil might be used for entrances and a blue for melody. Any scheme which the conductor chooses will do. Too many marks will, however, defeat their own purpose since they will cease to stand out. Some authorities insist that the conductor should have the smallest features of the score so well in mind that it is unnecessary to use marks of any sort.

Most full scores will have markings such as [A] , [B] , or ① ② at different intervals so as to facilitate finding the place when stops in rehearsal are necessary. These markings should be added to scores which do not have them and to all the individual parts of the ensemble, keeping the markings close together so that it will never be necessary to "count back" 20 measures from [C] etc. It is often advisable to number every measure, or at least every fifth measure, in both score and parts. This practice is a great time-saving device.

---

[1] Especially those published by Harcourt, Brace & Company.

Problems and Procedures

1. Practice playing the voice parts of choral scores in which each voice is on a separate staff, especially the four-part type in which the tenor is written in treble clef.

2. Practice reading string trios and quartets at the piano.

3. Practice playing from the full score at the piano, starting with the flute and oboe parts and then gradually adding transposing parts.

4. Take cornet, horn, and alto saxophone parts and read off the concert pitches represented by the notation.

5. Using a first violin part in which a clarinet solo is cued, read off the notes which the clarinetist is to read.

6. Do the same thing for the trombones and basses, reading from a solo cornet part.

7. Study several full band and orchestra scores so thoroughly that all important cues can be given by memory.

8. Have a violinist demonstrate for you all types of bowing, pizzicato, and con sordino.

Suggestions for Further Study

BERNSTEIN, M. *Score Reading,* M. Witmark & Sons, 1932.

BOULT, A. C. *The Technique of Conducting,* Hall the Printer, Ltd., Oxford, Section 7.

GAL, HANS. *Score Reading,* Weiner Philharmonischer Verlag A. G., Vienna, 1924.

GEHRKENS, K. W. *Essentials in Conducting,* Oliver Ditson Company, Inc., 1919, Chap. XI, Appendix B.

HEACOX, A. E. *Project Lessons in Orchestration,* Oliver Ditson Company, Inc., 1928, Lessons 9, 39.

SCHERCHEN, H. *Handbook of Conducting,* Oxford University Press, London, 1933, pp. 35-150.

STOESSEL, A. *The Technic of the Baton,* Carl Fischer, Inc., 1920, Chap. VI.

VAN BODEGRAVEN, P. "The Lost Chord", *Educational Music Magazine,* Vol. XVI, No. 1 (Sept.-Oct., 1936), p. 7.

WIER, ALBERT E. Miniature scores published by Harcourt, Brace & Company.

WOODS, G. H. *School Orchestras and Bands,* Oliver Ditson Company, Inc., 1919, Chap. 14, 15, 16.

CHAPTER FOUR

PLANNING THE REHEARSAL

There are a hundred and one details which must be carefully thought out before the actual rehearsal should begin. A first rehearsal, like a first impression, should attempt to create a favorable reaction. Rehearsals which move smoothly toward their objective from beginning to end are not a matter of chance; they are the result of hours of careful planning. In many schools, the rehearsal of a music group is attended by a bustle and confusion that would not be tolerated in any other department of the school. The playing and singing of such groups is usually just as careless and slipshod as the preliminary planning. The school music conductor must be an organizer, a teacher, and a conductor. At no time does his ability as an organizer make itself more manifest than it does when he carefully thinks through all of the details preliminary to the rehearsal.

Such details will vary in different situations and the solution of the problems created must be left to the individual ingenuity of the conductor. The young teacher may get some very valuable advice from his principal who should know conditions most thoroughly. The discussion which follows covers items of importance in pre-rehearsal planning and endeavors to stimulate the young conductor to discover other things of major or minor importance in his own school.

Selecting the Personnel

Selecting the personnel of the instrumental organizations will hardly create a problem, since the normal procedure is to include everyone who can play, at least, for the first few rehearsals. The unbalanced instrumentation which results may be corrected at least partially by shifting players to different instruments but this will be done after the first rehearsal.

One thing which should be done before the first rehearsal, if possible, and often it is not, is to hear each player individually. In small schools where there are few players, this is easy to do. It is necessary to know the individual ability of each player, in order to select the proper music for the first rehearsal. The exact number of players available and the instrument each plays must be known in order to make up music folios and decide on a seating arrangement.

Selecting the personnel of the vocal groups is a problem which must be thought through very carefully. In many schools, the practice is to have both selective and non-selective vocal groups. *There should be a*

53

large chorus in which anyone may sing, regardless of ability, and small groups into which only the best voices in the school are admitted. Such a plan is highly commendable because it gives everyone an opportunity to sing and also provides special opportunities for the more talented and experienced students.

Before voice tests are given, the conductor must decide what he will do with the unchanged and changing boys' voices, of which there will still be quite a number in the senior high school. These boys are usually permitted to sing in the non-selective chorus of mixed voices, while the selective groups are made up entirely of changed voices, although some conductors also use them in these groups. When assigning changing voices to parts, a good plan to follow is to place the boys where they can sing easily and then direct them to omit any tones which seem difficult. The voice which has started to drop may be assigned to the regular tenor part singing in the range of the changed tenor. Some practice is required to get the boys to sing an octave below the written part since they have been accustomed to singing soprano parts. These "boy tenors" must use their normal light head tones adding to the total effect of the tenors in quality of tone rather than in quantity. If such voices are used stridently, rough tones will result which will not blend with the regular tenor quality. Unchanged and changing boys' voices used in a mixed chorus should not be evident to the listener. Needless to say, such voices must be tested frequently and the possessors of them must be encouraged to seek a test when the range of the part they are singing becomes uncomfortable.

The voice test for members of the non-selective choral ensemble will need to determine *range* and *quality* so that the singer may be assigned to the proper part. The quality together with the range are the determining factors. A simple method of determining quality and range is to have the candidate sing an arpeggio in different parts of his voice. The conductor should try to hear, individually, every voice in the general chorus, for in this way he can discover both the weak members and the leaders. Moreover, students like to have the expert opinion of the conductor and are better satisfied with the parts assigned to them.

The tryouts of candidates for selective groups should be much more thorough and complete. These are the groups which are expected to do the highest quality of work, and improper selection of their personnel will defeat this goal even before a single rehearsal is held. The teacher giving the voice test must try to put each candidate at his ease so that he will be able to do his best. A short conversation before starting to sing will do much to create a friendly atmosphere and will also give the teacher a chance to hear the speaking voice of the candidate, which will give a hint as to the quality of the voice and indicate the approximate pitch on which the test should begin.

A most convenient way to keep a record of tests is to have some 4 x 6 cards printed with proper places for recording all information desired. On this card should be included: name, age, grade in school, type of voice, quality, range, power, intonation, diction, reading ability (if a test in sight-reading is given), previous experience in any field of music, remarks, and the date. The candidate may be given a numerical rating of 1 (excellent) to 5 (very poor) in each. Provision should be made to have enough space for several grades so that if a candidate is given a second or third test, the date of each can be recorded and the grades compared.

VOICE TEST

NAME _____ AGE _____

GRADE IN SCHOOL_____ TYPE OF VOICE_____

QUALITY_____ RANGE_____ POWER_____

INTONATION_____ DICTION_____ READING ABILITY_____

EXPERIENCE IN MUSIC _____

	FIRST TEST	SECOND TEST	THIRD TEST
DATE	_____	_____	_____
GRADE	_____	_____	_____

The test of these candidates can start with a familiar song with piano accompaniment, the candidate choosing the song. This song should then be repeated without accompaniment to see whether the singer can maintain the proper pitch from beginning to end. Next, the tester should strike a series of unrelated tones, asking the candidate to sing each tone immediately upon hearing it as a test for quick reaction to pitch. Range can be determined by downward scale vocalization, by an arpeggio, or by changing the pitch of the song sung until both bottom and top limits have been discovered.

Whether or not a reading test will be given depends upon the importance attached to such a test by the conductor and the musical background of the students. Such a test is obviously a waste of time when there has been little or no previous training in music reading.

When the tests have been completed and all information about each candidate has been obtained, the conductor is ready to choose the personnel of the group. He must then consider the following factors:

(1) *Tone Quality.* Is the quality such that it will blend with other voices? If the quality has defects, can these defects be easily eliminated by proper training?

(2) *Intonation.* The voice which is consistently below pitch should not be considered. Those voices which strike a tone on pitch but sing an occasional out-of-tune interval can usually be improved by interval drill. Since a few singers with poor intonation can pull down the entire ensemble and since correct intonation is the first requisite of good singing, the conductor cannot be too careful in his demands for accurate intonation from each individual singer.

(3) *Musical Background.* It is usual to give preference to students who have had previous experience in vocal music. This practice is a natural and logical one but there is a danger here that is not usually considered. We refer to the instance when two voices are about equal, but the one which has had no previous training is likely, with training, to develop into a better voice than the one which has already been trained. Persons with a background of instrumental experience but only fair voices, will add greatly to the ensemble by their leadership in reading music and their general musicianship. At least a few in each section may be given preference over students possessing better voices.

(4) *Diction, Power, Range.* These are important but can be materially improved by work in the ensemble and need not, therefore, be given major emphasis when making the final selections.

(5) *Balance.* Experience shows that balance is not obtained by selecting numerically balanced sections. Ten basses and ten tenors will not necessarily result in balanced men's voices, nor will ten sopranos balance ten basses. As a general rule the inside voices, that is the alto and tenor, can get along with fewer singers than the outer voices, the soprano and bass. Since real altos and tenors are a rarity in the senior high school this factor is of real importance. It is also quite possible that the female voices may outnumber the male voices two to one and still maintain an even balance. Balance then will be determined by the actual power of the voices placed in an ensemble rather than by any rigid numerical formula.

(6) Students who are finally selected may be picked because they do one of two things: they either add to the effectiveness of the ensemble,

or they do not detract from the final result. This is a rather negative way of putting it, but there will be many times when freshmen and sophomores are added to the ensemble not so much for what they will add but because they will do no harm and will be gaining experience so that during the following year they will make a contribution. Seniors should be chosen because they can make a real contribution. When two voices are about equal and a choice must be made, the forward-looking conductor will give preference to the younger candidate unless the older student has had previous experience in the ensemble.

(7) Candidates who are finally chosen for membership in the selected ensemble may be placed on probation for a trial period and should thoroughly understand this so that disappointments will be avoided. In spite of all the care which may be taken in tryouts, some voices will be admitted which will not fit into the ensemble and which will show other defects as time goes on. For the good of the entire ensemble, those voices must be dropped.

(8) It is a good practice to announce a group of alternates for each section. If any regular member needs to be dropped for any reason whatever, he can be replaced immediately by an alternate.

(9) When the teacher is well acquainted with each candidate, he will want to consider carefully the personality and temperament of the individual. An organization must have a good number of exuberant, enthusiastic members whose force and vitality will help immeasurably in creating "group spirit", so necessary to the successful functioning of any ensemble.

The teacher coming into a new school system for the first time must decide whether or not to require all old members of the ensemble to try out along with new candidates or whether to admit them without trial. It is recommended that a test be expected of everyone so that the teacher may know each voice more intimately, but if such a procedure seems to cause resentment among the old members the test might do more harm than good. Such seemingly trivial matters often are of great importance to the high school student and the sympathetic teacher will sense such a feeling and, when possible, compromise between the logical and psychological.

SELECTING THE MUSIC

It is impossible to overemphasize the tremendous importance of the selection of suitable music for each ensemble. The aims of the rehearsal, as presented in the next chapter, cannot be realized unless proper music has been selected. The job is complicated further by the fact that there is such a tremendous repertoire of music for choral and instrumental groups.

The following statement, discussing the selection of band music, pretty well sums up the problem for the choral and orchestral idioms as well:

> "Intelligent selection of music for any medium comes from extensive experience and knowledge of the whole field. The task is especially difficult for the band because we must rely largely upon transcriptions of orchestra scores; only recently has there appeared a greater number of concert compositions written directly for band. Thus, the bandmaster must know not only the value of the piece itself but also the relative value of various band arrangements. The task is further complicated in the school field by the necessity of choosing suitable material for several grades of organizations. No one person can be expected to be familiar with the whole repertoire. Therefore the band leader must rely upon the composite experience and knowledge of others as expressed in lists released by music teachers' associations and publishers."[1]

Evanson lists six points to be used as a basis for choosing high school vocal material:

> "1. Suitable text.
> 2. Really inspired music—variety of moods.
> 3. A cappella.
> 4. Right range for each section.
> 5. Each number fit into a well balanced program.
> 6. Must include numbers from every great source or school of choral music, and as many of the great composers as possible, so the course serves as a music appreciation course as well."[2]

Cain states:

> "I believe that the greatest success is had with the high school a cappella chorus when music appealing to the adolescent mind is used. It must be colorful, rich, romantic, and withal climactic."[3]

Mabelle Glenn gives the following points to be considered in choosing songs for a girls' song book:

> "1. Is the subject matter of the poem such that it will appeal to a girl in her early teens?
> 2. Has each melody sufficient charm to hold interest on its own account?

---

[1] G. R. Prescott and L. W. Chidester, *Getting Results with School Bands,* Paul A. Schmitt Music Company and Carl Fischer, Inc., 1938, p. 217.

[2] Jacob Evanson, "High School Choral Material," *Music Educators Journal,* Vol. XV, No. 5 (May, 1929), p. 51.

[3] Noble Cain, "What Kind of Music," *Music Educators Journal,* Vol. XVIII, No. 1 (Oct., 1931), p. 53.

3. Are the harmonies interesting without bringing any great difficulty to any part?
4. Is there a well defined highest point in each song where there is opportunity for a significant climax?
5. Does each song offer an opportunity for a wide range of dynamics?
6. Is there a good swing? Whether slow or fast, is there a decided rhythmic pulse?
7. Is there something of interest from the beginning to the end of each song?
8. When the melody ceases to be the outstanding element, is there something else to hold the interest of the listeners?
9. Is every selection well proportioned from an emotional standpoint? . . . Let us always remember that the words are the most important element in holding interest; therefore, they must be given every possible advantage in making the song an experience of beauty."[1]

The importance of selecting music which instrumental organizations can execute from a technical standpoint is made clear in the following statement by Carse:

"The school orchestra, however rudimentary its standard, will be a better musical educator for its members when the tone, ensemble and intonation are good, than when these are bad owing to totally inadequate technique; these essentially musical qualities are only possible of attainment when the music played lies within the range of the players' executive ability."[2]

In conclusion, it is safe to say that all music used in the public schools should:

1. Fit the ability of each section of the ensemble.
2. Hold the interest of the members of the ensemble.
3. Be conducive to finer technical and musical performance.
4. Be educational as well as entertaining.

SEATING ARRANGEMENTS

When the personnel and instrumentation of the ensemble is known to the conductor he can begin work on a temporary seating arrangement. This arrangement will vary with each group according to its size and

[1] Glenn, *Glee Club Book for Girls,* Oliver Ditson Company, Inc., 1928, as quoted by Mursell and Glenn, *The Psychology of School Music Teaching,* Silver Burdett Company, 1931, p. 282.
[2] A. Carse, *Orchestral Conducting,* Augener, Ltd., London, 1929, p. 28.

instrumentation. The conductor should experiment with various plans until he finds the one which best suits the group. It is well to divide the mixed chorus, regardless of size, into eight parts immediately, for then the chorus is arranged to sing six- or eight-part music and parts which occasionally divide.

Choral groups should be seated in a semi-circle so that each section can hear the other. The following plans for seating the mixed chorus are especially good when the girls greatly outnumber the boys.

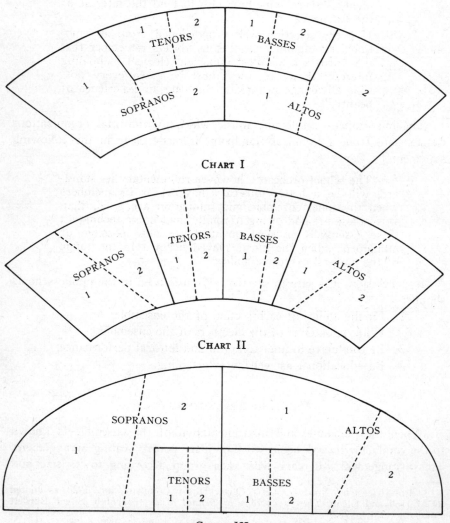

CHART I

CHART II

CHART III

The following seating plan for a full orchestra can be modified to suit smaller orchestras if the relative position of each instrument is maintained. In any size orchestra, the first violins are to the left of the conductor.

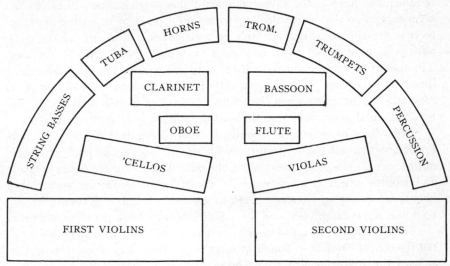

The seating arrangements for band are quite varied. In general, the trend from the military brass band to the symphonic band has tended to place the reeds in the front part of the band and the brass in the rear. The following arrangement is for a medium-sized band in which the reed players outnumber the brass players.

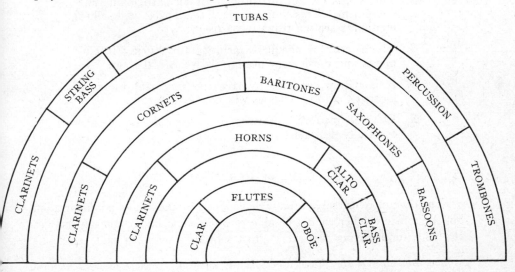

The Rehearsal Room

It is extremely unfortunate that many school administrators feel that the most important consideration in choosing a rehearsal room is that there be adequate floor space to accommodate the participants. They do not seem to realize that when dealing with sound, it is of utmost importance to consider the acoustical qualities of a classroom. The use of the gymnasium as a rehearsal room is a good example of this type of thinking. The use of a small room with bare, hard walls and no sound absorbing material is another. The assignment of music groups to such rooms is especially unfortunate when the auditorium is not in use or is being used by some small group which could work as efficiently in smaller quarters.

Regardless of where the rehearsal room is finally located, it is quite important that all music groups which are to appear in public, be permitted to hold frequent rehearsals in the auditorium. Inexperienced players and singers are easily confused by the differences in the sound they hear when changing from one room to another. The young conductor will have the same experience and the result can only be a poor performance.

The description of an ideal rehearsal room will not be attempted here[1], but the school conductor should attempt to convince his administration that at least the following five points be given consideration:

1. The acoustical properties of the room must be good. The conductor must be able to distinguish each section and individual at all dynamic levels. There must be no distortion of sound.

2. There must be adequate room for all participants and equipment. This implies that the space will allow legitimate seating plans to be used.

3. There must be adequate facilities for storing instruments and music very near to the rehearsal room.

4. It is highly desirable to have the rehearsal room so located that other classes will not be disturbed.

5. Elevated platforms or risers for ensemble groups are especially desirable.

Time of Rehearsal

The time of rehearsal is usually determined by the school administration but the music teacher should be able to offer some important suggestions. It goes without saying that every effort should be made to have rehearsals

---

[1] See *Bulletin No. 17*, "Music Rooms and Equipment," Music Educators National Conference, 1932.

during regular school hours. Quite often it is possible to have this done for all but one of the ensembles. In deciding which group should meet out of school hours, consideration should be given to the fact that members of the ensemble in which there is the most interest will probably attend rehearsals regardless of the time. Such an arrangement is, however, a compromise and not to be encouraged.

The time of rehearsal during the school day also should be given consideration. For obvious reasons, choral groups will not function well the first period after lunch. Many consider the last period in the morning to be the best for choral groups. The first period of the day is a good time for instrumental groups since it is often possible to start the rehearsals before the regular session begins and thus obtain more rehearsal time. Rehearsals held during the last period of the day can be extended after the close of school when necessary. Schools which have a regular assembly period often schedule the instrumental rehearsals the period before the assembly period so that the instrumental group can be prepared to play as the student body enters.

STUDENT OFFICERS

Most non-musical details of the rehearsal can be handled by student officers, leaving the conductor free to spend his time on the musical details. The number of student officers each group will have varies. The officers who play an important part in pre-rehearsal planning are the stage managers and librarians.

1. The Stage Managers

The duties of these officers are to see that all chairs, racks, and other equipment are in place before the rehearsal is scheduled to begin. To perform their duties, these officers must be free during the period preceding the rehearsal. The stage managers may be elected by members of the ensemble or appointed by the conductor.

2. The Librarians

The librarians place the music in the rehearsal folios and distribute these folios to their proper places as soon as the stage managers have finished their job. They collect the music at the close of the rehearsal, take care of issuing music for home practice, and are in complete charge of the music library. They should have a free period before the rehearsal. Much can be said in favor of appointing rather than electing the librarians, and in some way rewarding them for the tremendous amount of work they are called upon to do.

The easiest way to issue music for home practice is to place a large card inside each folio bearing the same number as the folio, on which each student may sign his name and the date the music is being taken. This card is then left on the rack and collected by the librarian. The same card is placed on the proper rack at the beginning of the next rehearsal period and the student signs the date he is returning the music and places the card back in the folio.

RULES AND REGULATIONS

Every member of an ensemble should be informed of the responsibilities he is accepting when entering the group. When rehearsals are held after or before regular school hours, it is particularly important that rules covering attendance be carefully drawn up. Groups which appear in public a great deal will save themselves a lot of trouble by insisting at the outset, that every member of the ensemble must be present on such occasions. The list of rules and regulations demanded in each locality should be printed and sent home to parents of the participants.

THE ACCOMPANIST

The conductor of a choral group who is a good pianist may often act as his own accompanist. At times, there seems to be no other solution, but when there is an accompanist available, it is usually better for the conductor not to do his own playing. By using an efficient accompanist he is freer to conduct and train his group. It is good education to use student accompanist whenever possible.

The music to be used in the first rehearsal should be given to the accompanist as long before the rehearsal as possible. The conductor will then have time to go over the music with the accompanist, indicating tempi, dynamics, and difficult places. The accompanist also must be trained to follow a conductor, to play parts, and harmonize vocalises; moreover, it is extremely valuable if he has the ability to transpose. An accompanist can make or break a rehearsal, so the conductor will want to give a great deal of time and thought to selecting and training a good one.

PROBLEMS AND PROCEDURES

1. In light of the aims of music education in the high school, if it were necessary for you to choose between scheduling the larger non-selective chorus or the smaller selective group, which would you favor? Give reasons for your answer.

2. Did your high school conductor choose music wisely? Justify your answer.

3. Draw seating plans for a chorus, band, and orchestra with which you are familiar. Point out the advantages and disadvantages of each.

4. Describe some rehearsal rooms which you have seen. How do they compare with the recommendations made in the M.E.N.C. *Bulletin No. 17* entitled "Music Rooms and Equipment"?

5. Do you think students should be permitted to take music out for home practice? Discuss some of the advantages and disadvantages.

6. Describe some musical organization with which you are familiar, and then draw up a list of rules and regulations for it. Defend each one.

7. Which student officers should be elected? Which appointed? Why?

Suggestions for Further Study

Beattie, McConathy and Morgan. *Music in the Junior High School,* Silver Burdett Company, 1930, pp. 165-169.

Bulletin No. 17, "Music Rooms and Equipment", Music Educators National Conference, 1932.

Cain, N. *Choral Music and Its Practice,* M. Witmark & Sons, 1932, Chap. VI, VII, VIII, Appendix I, II.

Christy, Van A. *Glee Club and Chorus,* G. Schirmer, Inc., 1940, Chap. II.

Gehrkens, K. W. *Essentials in Conducting,* Oliver Ditson Company, Inc., 1919, pp. 83, 95, 160, 147-151.

Glenn, M. "A New Goal in Ensemble Singing", *Music Educators Journal,* Vol. XV, No. 1 (Oct., 1928), p. 67. Suggestions for selection of music.

Krone and Wallace. "High School Students' Interest in Choral Music", *Music Educators Journal,* Vol. XXI, No. 2 (Oct., 1934), p. 26

Maddy and Giddings. *Instrumental Technique for Orchestra and Band,* Willis Music Co., 1926, pp. 39-43, 46-47, 10, 13, 63, 66.

Prescott and Chidester. *Getting Results with School Bands,* Paul A. Schmitt Music Company and Carl Fischer, Inc., 1938, Chap. XII, XIV, XVI.

Van Bodegraven, P. *Organizing a School Band,* Long Island City, New York: Penzel, Mueller & Co., 1938, pp. 45-46.

Williams, A. L. "Planning an Instrumental Rehearsal", *Music Educators Journal,* Vol. XVIII, No. 2 (Dec., 1931), p. 39.

Wilson, H. R. *Music in the High School,* Silver Burdett Company, 1941, Chap. XV.

CHAPTER FIVE

AIMS OF THE REHEARSAL

The conductor of any musical organization, be it choral or instrumental, amateur or professional, must have a well defined set of objectives towards which he is directing his group. Successful performances are not a matter of chance; they are the result of intelligent, long-range planning. The amateur musician often is led to believe that when he is playing or singing the correct notes and the correct rhythms he is functioning satisfactorily. This is not surprising since so many amateur rehearsals have only these two objectives. In this connection Evanson comments:

"At the end of a year the members know a few songs,
learned mostly by rote, but they have no definite training.
They have mastered no fundamental principles."[1]

The fundamental principles which he suggests are: the ability to read music; command of vocal technic (which includes breathing, development of a flowing tone, quality and pitch of the tone), good diction, and a correct interpretation.

Prescott and Chidester[2] list twenty-two full band rehearsal objectives among which are included: logical and artistic phrasings, accurate intonation, ensemble balance, sustained alertness, an accurate interpretation of the conductor's beat, sight reading, and general music appreciation.

Hollis Dann[3] considers the essential factors of good choral singing to be beautiful tone quality, superior diction, greatly increased and refined reading power, the emotional element developed and made vital, perfect attack and release, observance of dynamics, and artistic interpretation. If these factors constitute good choral singing they must also of necessity become objectives to be actively pursued during each rehearsal period.

ADJUDICATOR'S COMMENT SHEETS

The Adjudicator's Comment Sheets used by the National School Band, Orchestra and Vocal Association in all festivals sponsored by it give a very comprehensive picture of what school groups are judged on. The form used for vocal groups lists as major elements: interpretation and artistic effect, intonation, accuracy, rhythm, tone, diction, presentation, and

[1] J. Evanson, "Essentials of Better Choral Training", *Music Educators Journal*, Vol. XVII, No. 3 (February, 1931), p. 40.
[2] G. R. Prescott and L. W. Chidester, *Getting Results with School Bands*, Paul A. Schmitt Music Company and Carl Fischer, Inc., 1938, p. 99.
[3] H. Dann, "Essential Factors of Good Choral Singing," *Music Educators Journal*, Vol. XXII, No. 3 (Nov.-Dec., 1935), p. 17.

CHORAL GROUPS
ADJUDICATOR'S COMMENT SHEET
OFFICIAL FORM
NATIONAL SCHOOL VOCAL ASSOCIATION

ORDER OF APPEARANCE

CLASS.................

Name of Organization...

School.. City.................... State.........................

Numbers Sung: (1) Composer.................... Title................................

(2) Composer.................... Title................................

(3) Composer.................... Title................................

(Officials will grade principal items for each selection by inserting A, B, C, D or E in the squares opposite the items. Mark plus or minus (+ or. —) after the subdivisions which are noticeably good or noticeably poor. Two or more plus signs after an item indicate especially commendable work while two or more minus signs indicate decidedly poor work in that phase.)

INTERPRETATION & ARTISTIC EFFECT... ☐ ☐ ☐

Outstanding Strong Points:

Tempo ☐ ☐ ☐
Unity ☐ ☐ ☐
Contrast ☐ ☐ ☐
Proportion ☐ ☐ ☐
Phrasing:
　Attack ☐ ☐ ☐
　Release ☐ ☐ ☐
　Development ☐ ☐ ☐
　Melodic line ☐ ☐ ☐
Individuality ☐ ☐ ☐
Accompaniment ☐ ☐ ☐

INTONATION... ☐ ☐ ☐

Soprano ☐ ☐ ☐
Alto ☐ ☐ ☐
Tenor ☐ ☐ ☐
Bass ☐ ☐ ☐
Full ensemble ☐ ☐ ☐

ACCURACY... ☐ ☐ ☐

Notes ☐ ☐ ☐
Time values ☐ ☐ ☐
Dynamics ☐ ☐ ☐

RHYTHM... ☐ ☐ ☐

Outstanding Weak Points:

Too steady (check) ☐ ☐ ☐
Too free (check) ☐ ☐ ☐
Flow ☐ ☐ ☐

TONE... ☐ ☐ ☐

Quality ☐ ☐ ☐
Color ☐ ☐ ☐
Freedom ☐ ☐ ☐
Naturalness ☐ ☐ ☐
Balance ☐ ☐ ☐
Blend ☐ ☐ ☐
Quantity ☐ ☐ ☐
Control ☐ ☐ ☐

DICTION... ☐ ☐ ☐

Naturalness ☐ ☐ ☐
Purity of vowels ☐ ☐ ☐
Uniform vowel quality ☐ ☐ ☐
Consonants ☐ ☐ ☐

PRESENTATION... ☐ ☐ ☐

Sincere ☐ ☐ ☐
Convincing ☐ ☐ ☐
Faces reflect spirit of song ☐ ☐ ☐

APPEARANCE... ☐ ☐ ☐

Stage deportment ☐ ☐ ☐
Posture ☐ ☐ ☐

Recommended for: ....
(Division I, II, III, IV, V)

Signature of Official: ....

Copyright 1941 by National School Band, Orchestra and Vocal Associations, 64 E. Jackson Blvd., Chicago, Illinois. Used by permission.

V 7

ADJUDICATOR'S COMMENT SHEET
OFFICIAL FORM
NATIONAL SCHOOL BAND ASSOCIATION
NATIONAL SCHOOL ORCHESTRA ASSOCIATION

ORDER OF APPEARANCE

CLASS.........................

....

Name of Organization...

School.. City.................. State..................

Selections Played (1) March...

(2) Req. No. ....

(3) Sel. No. ....

(Officials will grade principal items for each selection by inserting A, B, C, D or E in the squares opposite the items. Mark plus or minus (+ or —) after the subdivisions which are noticeably good or noticeably poor. Two or more plus signs after an item indicate especially commendable work while two or more minus signs indicate decidedly poor work in that phase.)

GENERAL COMMENTS ON PERFORMANCE

TONE.................. 1 2 3 □ □ □

	1	2	3
Beauty........			
Smoothness ...			
Control.......			
Richness......			
Balance.......			
Volume.......			

(BAND)
MARCH □
(Mark A, B, C, D or E)

INTONATION........... 1 2 3 □ □ □

	1	2	3
Strings.........			
Reeds.........			
Brasses........			
Individuals....			

(ORCHESTRA)
STRING NUMBER □
(Mark A, B, C, D or E)

INTERPRETATION...... 1 2 3 □ □ □

	1	2	3
Phrasing......			
Style.........			
Dynamics.....			
Expression....			
Tradition.....			
Tempo........			
Rhythm.......			
Accent........			

REQUIRED COMPOSITION □
(Mark A, B, C, D or E)

TECHNIQUE............. 1 2 3 □ □ □

	1	2	3
Precision......			
Fluency.......			
Articulation...			
Bowing.......			

SELECTED COMPOSITION □
(Mark A, B, C, D or E)

GENERAL EFFECT...... 1 2 3 □ □ □

	1	2	3
Spirit.........			
Sincerity.....			
Taste.........			
Contrast.....			

Outstanding strong points:

STAGE DEPORTMENT.. 1 2 3 □ □ □

	1	2	3
Discipline.....			
Appearance....			

Outstanding weak points:

INSTRUMENTATION.... 1 2 3 □ □ □

	1	2	3
Strings........			
Reeds.........			
Brass.........			
Percussion....			

Recommended for: ....
(Division I, II, III, IV, V)

Signature of Official...

BO 1

appearance with subdivisions under each major head. The instrumental form has as its major elements: tone, intonation, interpretation, technic, general effect, stage deportment, and instrumentation, each with subdivisions.

The Adjudicator's Comment Sheets for the National Competition-Festivals have been presented on pages 68 and 69 for a two-fold reason: (1) If a director plans to participate in any of the district, state, regional, and national contests, he will be able to check the performance of his group against the points on which it will be judged at the contests; (2) even though a school music conductor does not plan to participate in any organized contest, it is well for him to keep in mind a check list such as the one presented in these adjudication sheets, against which he can continually measure the performance of his group.

These illustrations make it obvious that the conductor must give some attention to all of the elements which go to make up a satisfactory musical performance. Now let us consider briefly the most important of these elements. A discussion of procedures to be used in realizing these aims will be discussed in the chapters following.

TECHNICAL ACCURACY

Technical accuracy in music refers to such things as playing or singing the correct pitches, giving each tone the exact number of beats indicated by the printed page, using correct bowings, articulations, and the like. The conductor of any school group will find that a great part of his time must be spent in attempting to obtain technical accuracy. Until at least a reasonable amount of accuracy is attained, a real musical performance is out of the question. *However, it must be also understood that a correct technical performance is by no means necessarily a musical one.*

INTONATION

The importance of playing and singing in tune is so obvious that special mention of it seems unnecessary here. It may be well to point out that even the uneducated listener is able to detect faults in intonation, and that no one is able to enjoy a musical performance which is consistently out of tune.

The school music conductor must of necessity spend a great deal of time during each rehearsal period on intonation problems. The amateur musician with none too good an ear and an uncertain control of his instrument will not play or sing in tune, unless he is continually made conscious of the need for doing so and also is given a great deal of help.

Tone Quality

Beautiful tone quality is one of the most satisfying elements of a good musical performance. A tone which is in tune will not detract from a performance, unless it is raucous or strident, but if it is to make a positive contribution it must have quality. When an ensemble starts to produce tones which are in tune and have a satisfying tone quality, then the ensemble is well on the road to providing a satisfying musical experience for both participants and listeners.

The conductor must consciously and continually strive to obtain good tone quality from the ensemble. If this important element is left to chance it will never be obtained.

Balance and Blend

An ensemble is a group of musicians playing or singing together. The big difference between this and solo performance is that there are many more parts present, some of more importance than others, and that all of these parts must make an intelligible whole. A powerful bass section can ruin a choir unless its power is cut down to the level of the weaker sections. The brass and percussion sections of a band can, and often do, spoil the performance of the band by overpowering the weaker reed section. In other words, there must be balance both between sections and within sections so that melodies are properly supported by the accompaniment and so that each note of a chord is given the right amount of volume.

Such balance cannot be left to the discretion of immature high school musicians. When they are properly trained, they will learn to listen for these things and will appreciate their importance. *But in the initial stages it will be a survival of the loudest unless the conductor gives the problem of balance full attention.*

The problem of securing blend usually occurs within a section when one singer or player does not blend in with the rest of the section. The effect of the entire section may be spoiled by one individual so that the problem of blending becomes of great importance. Each member of a section must be taught to listen to see if he is blending properly. This problem is closely related to the one of securing good tone quality since it is often a flaw in tone quality which results in poor blend.

Coordinated Ensemble

The conductor is responsible for making the group under his direction perform as an integrated unit. This means that the members of an ensemble must understand the signals used by the conductor and must be alert to respond to them. By carefully watching the conductor and listening keenly, every member is able to work as part of a coordinated ensemble. All attacks, releases, and tempo changes will be performed exactly together.

DICTION

Diction is a particular problem of choral groups which many conductors seem to neglect because, as they say, everyone can speak English and we should sing as we speak. It is not as easy as that! The weird sounds which are the result of this theory should prove to a discriminating ear that problems of diction are of major importance. Pure vowel sounds and initial and final consonants are not obtained by chance. They are obtained by diligent work on them at every rehearsal.

INTERPRETATION

An organization which performs the mechanics of music correctly, has good intonation and fine tone quality, maintains a perfect balance and blend, and uses excellent diction has all the necessary qualifications to produce excellent musical results. It now requires a conductor who can utilize these qualifications to their fullest advantage by giving the music being studied the finest interpretation possible. The emphasis here must be on creating, by means of tempo, phrasing, and dynamics, the exact emotional reaction required to make the music live. Unless this emotional release is obtained, it will be hard to justify the many values claimed for music in our educational system.

ORDER OF PROCEDURE

It is difficult to point out one of the foregoing elements in good musical performance and insist that it must come before all others but it does seem as though some elements must be emphasized before others. Carse writes:

> "The following is suggested as the order in which faults should be attacked: first get the tune right . . . and so get the body to move roughly together; then tackle the wrong notes, and so reduce the tonality to some sort of order; after that the worst of the faulty intonation might have some attention . . . Finally, the light and shade, expression and a few more delicate adjustments can be made . . . It is wasteful to spend much time on refinements and subtleties when the general standard of executive ability is low."[1]

In speaking of the processes which occur in music reading, Maddy and Giddings[2] suggest as the proper order: (1) the production of tone;

[1] A. Carse, *Orchestral Conducting*, Augener, Ltd., London, 1929, pp. 28, 29.
[2] J. E. Maddy and T. P. Giddings, *Instrumental Technique*, The Willis Music Company, 1926, p. 7.

(2) playing in tune; (3) accurate reading of notes; (4) attention to expression. In reading vocal music the sequence would be tone, time, pitch, words, and expression.

It should be noted that both of the above suggestions refer to working out of a piece of music for the first time and are not concerned with the long range improvement of the ensemble.

Bakaleinikoff states:

> "The existence of music is for pleasure, and bad intonation always gives displeasure even for the ordinary listener; therefore, intonation must always occupy *first place*."[1]

Lyravine Votaw holds the same belief as is shown in the following statement:

> "True intonation is the largest factor in acceptable choral singing. Without it, the finest tonal picture, the most perfect interpretation, the purest vowel formation, the clearest enunciation of consonants, the most skillful baton technic count for naught."[2]

The following statement by Richard Wagner would lead to the belief that tone control must be acquired before much real interpretation can be attempted:

> "Yet tone sustained with equal power is the basis of all expression, with the voice as with the orchestra; the manifold modifications of the power of tone, which constitute one of the principal elements of musical expression, rest upon it."[3]

The obvious conclusion to be drawn from these quotations is that consideration must be given to the technic of music, note values, pitches, tone, and intonation before much can be done with interpretation. At the same time it might be well to point out that technic develops from early attempts at interpretation. Technic and expression grow side by side.

It can also be seen how dependent a good musical performance is on all of the elements listed. Take any one of them out and the performance becomes unsatisfactory. A group which plays in tune but with poor tone may be less irritating than one which plays out of tune with good tone quality, but neither group is producing a pleasing result. It is probably true that a conductor often enters the rehearsal room determined to emphasize one element above all others, but he will soon find that each element must have some attention if musical results are to be obtained.

---

[1] V. Bakaleinikoff, *Elementary Rules of Conducting*, Belwin, Inc., 1938, p. 25.
[2] L. Votaw, "Choral Intonation", *Music Educators Journal*, Vol. XVII, No. 1 (Oct., 1931), p. 50.
[3] R. Wagner, *On Conducting*, William Reeves, London, 1919, p. 32.

PROBLEMS AND PROCEDURES

1. Suggest some aims for the rehearsal, other than those presented in this chapter. Discuss them.

2. Would you consider the improvement of reading music to be a major aim of the rehearsal? Justify your answer. Describe procedures you would take for developing the reading power of choral groups.

3. In your experience with high school groups, which of the aims listed in this chapter are least satisfactorily realized? What is the explanation of this?

4. Do you think the band is the type of organization which should have a lower standard of musical performance and therefore a different set of rehearsal aims than the orchestra or chorus? Why?

5. Describe a high school concert you have attended in which a mixed chorus, orchestra, and band appeared. Which organization seemed to most fully realize the aims of good musical performance as set up in this chapter? Compare your statements with those of students who have attended other concerts. Does any one type of school music ensemble seem to have higher performing standards than others?

SUGGESTIONS FOR FURTHER STUDY

Read the complete articles or chapters from which references in this chapter have been taken.

The bibliography for Chapters Six and Seven may be used for this chapter also.

CHAPTER SIX

THE CHORAL REHEARSAL

Many high schools do not have special voice classes. Students are admitted directly into one of the large vocal ensembles without having had any special training beyond the singing done in the elementary school. Even such training loses much of its value for the boys, because their voices have altered so much that they feel as though they are singing with a new instrument as, indeed, they are. If a good foundation in music reading, breath management, diction, and other elements of good singing has been formed in the pre-high school vocal work, the high school conductor is indeed fortunate. This is so rarely true, however, that the conductor would do well to plan his work as though starting with an inexperienced group and then make those modifications which seem necessary as the ensemble progresses.

As has already been indicated in the preceding chapter, the type of rehearsal procedure here favored is one which lays a solid foundation built upon the fundamentals of correct singing. Such a foundation will assure an ever-increasing mastery of fundamentals and a progressively higher degree of musical performance. The rehearsal in which no attention is given to the fundamentals of voice production may result in a slightly improved grade of singing just because of the time put in; but it may just as easily lead to a poorer grade of singing because of the constant repetition of incorrect vocal habits. However, the rehearsal in which correct vocal fundamentals are given some attention should lead to a progressively higher type of singing. The following statement by the Adolescent Voice Committee of the American Academy of Teachers of Singing emphasizes this viewpoint:

> "We believe that notwithstanding the significance and benefits of mass singing and the need for it, the primary stress in the early years should be on the correct use of the voice. This will not necessarily be brought about by mass singing. In fact, all too often the contrary is true; the stress on effects from the group—with little regard to the use of the voice—generally proves antagonistic to the vocal welfare of the singer. We submit that only through sufficient attention to the correct use of the voice may the joy of singing, the chief aim of mass singing, be fully realized. It is axiomatic to say that a certain degree of skill in any physical endeavor is necessary for any considerable degree of success."[1]

---

[1] "A Statement of Principles", *Music Educators Journal,* Vol. XXV, No. 3 (Dec., 1938), p. 26.

If we accept the premise that fundamentals must be taught in the large choral ensemble, it becomes evident that there will be a great deal of similarity between the small voice class and the large ensemble in respect to the principles of voice to be covered. In the small voice class a great deal of attention can be given to each individual while in the large ensemble this is not possible. Since the success of a large ensemble is dependent primarily upon the individual ability of its members one of the weaknesses of teaching fundamentals in a large group is that insufficient attention can be given to each member. The degree of thoroughness with which each point can be gone into is another big difference between the voice class and the large ensemble. These two big drawbacks to teaching fundamentals in the large ensemble as opposed to teaching them in voice classes are given only to indicate that the voice class is the ideal foundation for large ensemble singing. Lacking ideal conditions, many of the fundamentals of singing must be taught in the large ensemble rehearsal.

Mastery of voice fundamentals is, of course, only a means to an end the end being the correct rendition of any song. What this means is made clear by Carol Pitts when she writes:

> "A thorough technical foundation is essential to an artistic interpretation of music, for it is impossible for a voice to respond to demands made upon it if it is not under the control of the singer. What then, are the demands made upon the singer?
>
> 1. Absolute control of the tone as to pitch, volume, and quality.
> 2. Ability to sustain a tone for as long as may be necessary without its wavering in pitch, color, or intensity.
> 3. Ability to sing easily with pleasing color, without a break or change in quality, without "flatting" and with full resonant tones through the entire range of the voice.
> 4. Ability to crescendo a tone from pianissimo to triple forte and likewise to descrescendo, without "squeezing" the throat muscles, "swallowing" the tone, changing tonal quality, or wavering in pitch.
> 5. Ability to sing a vibrant, ringing tone, full of warmth and resonance, without harshness, and to sing the softest pianissimo without it becoming anaemic and lifeless.
> 6. Ability to sing all vowels with pure, beautiful tone quality, and, in addition, to form the consonantal sounds of the English language clearly and distinctly without disturbance of the vowel."[1]

---

[1] C. Pitts, *Pitts Voice Class Method,* Neil A. Kjos Music Co., 1936, p. 2.

This emphasis upon voice fundamentals is in keeping with the aims of the rehearsal as enumerated in the preceding chapter. It is one thing to set up aims and another thing to achieve them. It is easy to say that good tone quality and intonation are highly desirable but it is not so easy to obtain them. Merely realizing vaguely that they are important is not enough. A definite plan of obtaining them should be formulated and successfully carried out. Therefore, let us consider these aims and suggest a few of the many ways of realizing them.

TONE QUALITY[1]

A ringing resonant tone is dependent upon the free coordination of all the vocal muscles and organs used in producing a tone. Correct posture is one of the first considerations in producing a tone for it enables the vocal muscles to act freely. A good standing posture is one in which the feet are slightly apart with one foot ahead of the other and the weight of the body resting largely on the balls of the feet and distributed evenly between them. The body is erect with the chest normally high, but not strained. The head is in a natural position, neither thrown back nor pulled down toward the chest; the arms hang easily at the sides and the hands are clasped loosely in front of the waist. The body should not feel stiff nor should it slump. The sitting posture should maintain this erect position for the upper part of the body, which means that the back does not touch the chair, unless the back of the chair is so constructed that correct sitting posture is possible with the back of the singer touching it. The conductor must insist upon correct standing and sitting postures until they become habitual with the members of the group.

The vowel is the key to beautiful tone production. Correct singing of vowels unlocks the vocal mechanism and opens the way to proper management of the breath, unimpeded vibration of the vocal cords or folds, and free resonance. The one most apparent fault in the singing of members of high school choral groups is a rigid jaw. Much of the dark and covered, as well as the pinched and throaty tone production that is heard can be traced to this fault. Get their mouths open! Give the tone a chance! Correct vowel production, as well as diction, is dependent upon a free, open jaw, mobile lips, and a flexible tongue. Sing each vowel several times on each pitch of various descending scales. Roll an r after the vowels ah, oh, and ay to keep them open and bright. Introduce ee and oo with m to keep them round. Treble voices should open their mouths long when singing ee and oo in the upper voice. They should round the lips slightly when singing these vowels in the middle and lower part of the voice to keep tone quality from being thin. After vocalizing on single vowels, then combine vowels. The following two exercises can be used as a basis for all vowel study:

---

[1] See H. R. Wilson, *The Solo Singer*, Carl Fischer, Inc., 1941.

1.

are, are, are, are, are, are, are, are, are, are, are, are,
or, or, or, or, or, or, or, or, or, or, or, or,
air, air, air, air, air, air, air, air, air, air, air, air,
mee, mee, mee, mee, mee, mee, mee, mee, mee, mee, mee, mee,
moo, moo, moo, moo, moo, moo, moo, moo, moo, moo, moo, moo,
are, ee, are, ee, are, ee, are, ee, are, ee, are, ee,
or, air, or, air, or, air, or, air, or, air, or, air,
oo, ee, oo, ee, oo, ee, oo, ee, oo, ee, oo, ee,
are, air, are, air, are, air, are, air, are, air, are, air,

2.

are, are, are, are, are,	are, are, are, are, are,
or, or, or, or, or,	or, or, or, or, or,
air, air, air, air, air,	air, air, air, air, air,
mee, mee, mee, mee, mee,	mee, mee, mee, mee, mee,
moo, moo, moo, moo, moo,	moo, moo, moo, moo, moo,
are, or, are, or, are,	are, or, are, or, are,
or, air, or, air, or,	or, air, or, air, or,
oo, ee, oo, ee, oo,	oo, ee, oo, ee, oo,

Good tone production is dependent upon the proper management of the breath, but to begin the study of singing with long discussions about breath is usually confusing and misleading to the student. As the vowel is the key to beautiful tone production, so breath is the lock which must be opened before beautiful tone production is possible.

There are only two principles which choral singers need to know about breath action to meet all of the demands made upon their voices. The first is that of inhalation. A deep breath is necessary to prepare the body for the coordinated muscular act of singing. When one breathes deeply, there will be an expansion of the muscles around the waistline. Breathe through the mouth, for that is the way one must breathe while singing. There should not be a feeling of "lifting" the body, but rather, a feeling of "resting" the torso on the hips.

The act of inhalation is getting ready to sing and is very important. The act of exhalation produces tone and bears a close relationship to inhalation. The body should retain the feeling of "resting down", for this gives support to the tone. *Do not try to control the breath by holding it back.* Such effort will only cause one to lose more breath. Don't worry about the action of the diaphragm or about the stomach pulling in or pushing out. One often hears the statement "Sing with the breath". It is the same thing as saying "Breathe into the tone". Breath support will come through the feeling of "resting the tone down", and breath control will result from the feeling of a continuous stream of breath into the tone.

If vowels can be produced correctly and breath properly managed, beautiful tones will result. When the articulators are so free that they do not interfere with the vocal act, a legato and singing line can be retained.

A good singing tone, then, has three important characteristics:

(1) *A good tone is free.* This means that there is no muscular interference, that is, no tension of the neck, throat, jaw, or tongue muscles. A relaxed jaw and open mouth should be especially emphasized for it is a requisite of free tone production. It is often neglected by the boys who have a tendency to thrust their jaws forward and up, a certain indication of tension in the jaw, neck, and throat muscles.

A tone which is free really feels free. This feeling may be attained first on tones in the middle part of the voice. As soon as the physical conditions for singing these tones freely can be established, the voice can be carried to the high and low extremes immediately. Do not neglect range too long. It is one of the tests of a free tone. If the high notes of tenors and other voices do not come, then the production is not free and the conductor or teacher may well check his method and procedure.

As in the case of range, the free physical action of singing can best be established when singing *mf* tones in the middle part of the voice. As soon as these tones seem free the extremes in dynamics, both *ff* and *pp*, should be attempted and developed. There is no doubt that very loud strained singing will hurt voices, but the anaemic singing of the a cappella choirs in many of our high schools will equally impair voices for expressive singing. A free voice has a ringing *forte* as well as a shimmering *piano*. If his choir cannot sing loudly with a free quality, as well as softly, the conductor had again better check his voice method and procedure.

To gain freedom it is well to practice flexible exercises and study flexible songs. Flexibility is so often neglected by conductors and voice teachers. There is a high correlation between flexibility and quality. The flexible voice is a free voice. The free voice is a beautiful voice.

(2) *A good tone is resonant.* A resonant tone is practically the same thing as saying that it is free. A resonant tone rings. It is not dark and throaty, nor pinched and thin. There is a center to a resonant tone; it is not hollow.

The best way to develop resonance is through the study of vowels until the action of the breath and vocal cords is coordinated with the resonance cavities. Humming develops a feel of resonance, although it is doubtful if it is as valuable for developing resonance as open vowels, such as *ah* and *oh*. Fast humming exercises are excellent for the development of freedom which is probably the best recommendation of humming as a resonance builder.

(3.) *A good tone is expressive.* A voice that is expressive has a personal quality in it. The emotional reaction of the singer to the music is reflected in the tone. Today one hears considerable about subjective and objective tone quality. Subjective tone quality is the expressive and personal element but it is made possible by an understanding of the principles of voice production and the ability to put them into practice. The latter is the objective element of tone quality. High school singers, to make their voices expressive, must be encouraged and inspired to sing with abandon and enter into the spirit of music with "all their hearts." Melodious songs with noble sentiment and appealing texts must be used if inspirational singing from these young adults is to be obtained.

The three requirements of good tone quality, that it be free, resonant, and expressive will best be appreciated and understood by the student if he is enabled to hear a tone which has these characteristics. The singing of the teacher, other students, and recording and radio artists make this feasible. Such practice can be called teaching by imitation or it can be thought of as building correct concepts. If the students are encouraged to imitate someone's tone, certain dangers must be guarded against. The characteristics of freedom, resonance, and expressiveness are to be imitated but not the timbre or tone quality itself. The demonstrating voice may have a tenor quality which a bass, alto, or soprano may not want to imitate. The individualistic quality of each voice should be maintained.

If good tone quality is to be developed in any choral group, music for the ensemble must be chosen with regard to three essentials:

(1.) The range of the music should be comfortable for each section. Singing tones which are not within comfortable range cause tension and strident tone quality as well as poor intonation. It is possible to develop wide ranges in high school voices, but until they are so developed, care must be taken in the selection of music.

It will often be found that the tenor part contains notes which are too high to be sung easily in full voice. It is imperative that high school boys learn to use half-voice proficiently and to use it on all upper tones which would otherwise cause tension. Half-voice utilizes what is left of the man's child voice and is often called *falsetto*. It produces an effortless tone and can be developed to have good carrying power. A good way to rediscover this voice is to sing the vowel *oo* in the middle register, say G, mezzo-forte and then sing the G above, softly.

②. Much of the music should be of the sustained, legato type. Sustained tone forms the basis of all good singing and music should be used which demands it. Much of the early sacred music is of this type and is ideal for tonal development. It also calls for the singing of long phrases, demanding proper breath management. However, don't make a fetish of 16th and 17th Century music for these modern 20th Century young people. Don't neglect the music of Brahms or contemporary composers.

③. The music should be inspirational. It should be of such value that the ensemble will enjoy singing it and will respond with a wholesome emotional reaction. If there is no emotional reaction, there is poor tone quality.

INTONATION

In most high school choral rehearsals it is necessary to spend much of the time correcting faulty intonation. There is no one element upon which good singing is more dependent than upon good intonation. The job of the conductor is twofold. He must first analyze the difficulty and find the reason for out-of-tune singing, and second, he must prescribe treatment which will correct the mistakes. Some of the most frequent reasons for poor intonation found in high school choral organizations and suggested remedies follow. As the conductor gains in experience, he will invent remedies of his own since a variety of methods of attack are always more satisfactory than any single plan.

①. *Lack of proper breath management, faulty vowel formation, and inflexible articulation* are probably the most common causes of poor intonation with young singers. These causes can be remedied by following continually the procedures already suggested for development of tone. Thus, work on tone and intonation proceed hand in hand.

②. *Incorrect hearing of the interval to be sung is another major cause of poor intonation.* Our system of tonality has become so thoroughly imbedded in our minds that we sometimes forget it is a man-made system and that young singers need a great deal of help to comprehend it thoroughly. Each interval represented in music must be played and then sung until the proper sound is memorized. Certain faults will appear so often that the conductor is justified in expecting them to be present and therefore to attack them at their first appearance. One of these faults is that ascending intervals are sung too small and descending intervals too large, therefore the ensemble must consciously attempt to hear ascending intervals as being larger and descending intervals as being smaller. The ascending and descending half-steps are particular offenders in this respect. It also will be found that certain degrees of the scale give more difficulty than others. This is particularly true of the third and sixth degrees and the

* Inertia — a tendency to remain in a fixed condition.
If moving, to keep moving in the same direction, unless
affected by some outside force.
82   THE SCHOOL MUSIC CONDUCTOR

ensemble must be trained consciously to think these degrees high when
singing ascending passages. When singing a series of *REITERATED* reiterated pitches
the tendency is to sing each succeeding pitch slightly flat. The conductor
may correct this fault by suggesting that the ensemble sing succeeding
pitches slightly sharp. In this manner correct intonation is obtained.

(3.) *Mental and physical inertia are major causes of poor intonation.*
Mental inertia may be induced by the use of uninspirational music, an inert
conductor, or mental laziness on the part of members of the ensemble. A
fast moving rehearsal, in which everyone is busily at work and enjoying
it, will dispel much of this trouble, but the conductor must always be on
his guard against *"inertia."* Attention and concentration must be expected
and achieved.

Physical inertia may be caused by the temperature and air in the
room, rehearsing after lunch or at the end of a fatiguing day, an epidemic
of colds, or a touch of spring fever. If the air in the room is fresh and the
temperature around 68°, a few deep breaths will often help to stimulate
and refresh the singers and conductor. Nevertheless, there will be days
when the rehearsal seems to proceed in reverse, sometimes so much so that
it might be better to declare a holiday.

(4.) *Faulty hearing may be a cause for poor intonation,* particularly
in groups where tryouts have not been thorough enough to eliminate
the habitual out-of-tune singer. The person who has defective hearing will
not be able to match pitches perfectly. The pitch sung will usually be lower
than the one struck on the piano and the singer will not be conscious of it.
When the defect is not too serious it sometimes can be partially corrected
by placing the person in front of some strong voices so that the correct
pitch is being continually sung into his ear. However, singers with good
ears often find it difficult to keep on pitch when a flat-singer is near, because
their ears are sensitive to pitch deviation, while the out-of-tune singer is
often oblivious to the pitches being sung by others. Certainly the ensemble
which admits many singers with defective hearing is inviting poor
intonation.

(5.) *The music being studied may be the cause of poor intonation.* Music
which demands extreme ranges and dynamics may cause forcing and tension resulting in poor tone and intonation. Music which moves faster
than the singer can manipulate his vocal mechanism results in loss of control of tone and intonation. It is also true that certain ensembles can sing a
number perfectly in tune in one key while they may sing out of tune in
another key. Unaccompanied numbers particularly should be sung in a
variety of keys. Repetition of a number in the same key day after day
leads to inertia and poor intonation. Flatting may often be corrected by
raising the pitch of the song a half-step.

Choral ensembles should practice both with and without the piano if good intonation is to be achieved. In the preliminary stages, the piano may be depended on to furnish the correct measurement of pitch. As more skill is developed the ensemble will depend less and less on this aid and will rely more on a developed grasp of tonality and chordal blend. Unaccompanied singing is particularly valuable since it puts the burden of singing in tune entirely on the ear, but if the student has not learned or been trained to listen carefully, intonation may be particularly bad and it can be remedied most quickly by comparison with some mechanical pitch such as that of the piano. An ensemble which has developed good intonation can sing in tune with or without the accompaniment.

BALANCE

Discriminate listening must be developed to a high degree in order to obtain a proper balance of parts. Balance can be obtained only if each section hears every other section. A seating arrangement which makes this possible should be used. Ensemble work of any kind implies teamwork and the lack of it will result in poor balance immediately. The soloist who has fine tone quality and sings perfectly in tune may need considerable training before he can become an accomplished ensemble performer. It takes experience to be able to determine how much or how little volume it is necessary to use in order to maintain a proper balance of parts. The conductor is relied upon a great deal in maintaining a correct balance. The performers learn to expect a warning when they sing too strongly or too weakly. This is particularly true when giving a performance in a strange hall since every hall has acoustical problems of its own which only the conductor in front of the ensemble can fully appreciate.

Judgment must be developed with respect to determining the relative importance of a part or note of a chord. Most choral music has the same dynamic marking in each part but it soon becomes evident that following this literally will result in poor balance since both melody and accompaniment will be given the same importance. Lack of balance in a chord becomes evident when the root and fifth are sung louder than the third or seventh. There are often twice as many singers on one tone of a chord as there are on the other tones and if the group does not listen and use discrimination a definite lack of balance will result.

Singers should learn to recognize which tone of a chord they are singing. A little work on sustained chords taken from a number being studied will allow the members of the ensemble to hear how chords are built and to judge the relative importance of each tone. There is a joy in listening to a well balanced chord. The harmonic element in music has a great appeal for high school students and they enjoy singing and listening to chords.

There also must be balance within a section. The singer with the most power often stands out and creates poor balance but this is just as often the fault of the timid singer whose weakness emphasizes his partner's strength. A singer who overpowers the rest of his section is guilty of over-balancing the section but the singer who stands out because of some peculiarity in tone quality is offending in respect to blend.

BLEND

There are some singers whose tone quality is difficult to blend into an ensemble. This is often due to an excessively large vibrato or to nasality which may give a harsh, piercing quality to the voice. These singers should be cautioned not to sing as loudly as the other members of the section. When toned down in this manner the unpleasant quality of their voices is greatly reduced and will be absorbed by the mellowness of the other singers. Each individual voice will add a characteristic color to the ensemble tone but the resulting colors must blend.

Voices should first be blended within each section and then the various sections should be blended together. Work on sustained intervals, particularly the major and minor thirds, will help greatly. The importance of blend can be illustrated by working with two individuals, one of whom has a tendency to stand out. When the ensemble hears the defect the members will consciously attempt to modify their own voices to blend with those of their neighbors. A little work in this manner using various vowel sounds will illustrate that good diction and blend are closely related.

DICTION

Group singing implies teamwork and teamwork demands uniform action. Good diction is an absolute essential in choral singing and good diction in ensemble singing means uniform diction as well. Soloists may have slightly different ways of making certain vowel sounds, both good, but ensemble singers should adopt the sounds set up by the conductor. The emphasis in school work has been upon naturalness in diction but due to present practices of slovenly speech this often results in poor diction.[1]

One of the greatest difficulties with singers is that they know the sound they are attempting to sing and, therefore, feel certain that they are producing the correct tone. They do not listen to the tone and the result is the incoherent babbling prevalent at many choral performances.

---

[1] See Appendix B for suggestions concerning pronunciation of Latin.

There are several phases of diction which should have the direct attention of conductors:

1. Vowels

In singing, vowels perform a double duty. First of all, they serve as the means for sustaining the tone, and secondly, they contribute, together with the consonants, to the understanding of the word. The conductor should illustrate how each vowel should sound and then have the ensemble imitate it. Lip and tongue muscles should work actively. Mouths should open freely. It is fun for the conductor to form the various vowels silently with the lips and then to have the ensemble guess the vowel which is being formed. Students may practice this device among themselves. Do not hesitate to exaggerate the formation of each vowel sound.

2. Initial Consonants

It is by means of consonants that words are understood. Choral groups may sing perfect vowels, but unless the consonants are clear and distinct the words will not be understood. Flexibility in the enunciation of initial consonants can be secured by singing fast descending vocalises, such as the exercise on page 86, using the vowel *ah* with each consonant of the alphabet. In pronouncing the different consonants the tongue, the lips, and the jaw are used to varying degrees. It may be well to classify the consonants according to the physical movement needed to pronounce them in singing with the vowel *ah*.

> *b, m, p*—lip movement, very little jaw movement
> *d, l, n, t*—tip of tongue movement, little or no jaw movement
> *c* (hard), *g* (hard), *k*—middle of tongue movement, little or no jaw movement
> *c* (soft), *g* (soft), *j, s, y, z*—mostly jaw movement, some tongue movement
> *h*—open mouth, diaphragm movement
> *q*—lip, tongue, and jaw movement
> *r*—tip of tongue slightly rolled
> *w*—jaw and lip movement

3. Final Consonants

Some conductors give much time to initial consonants but give little thought to final consonants. To prove the importance of the final consonant in diction the conductor need only sing some vowel beginning with an initial consonant, and while he is holding the vowel ask the members of the ensemble to guess silently what word he is pronouncing. After he has finished singing the word, find out the number in the group who guessed the right word, and also, other words which the group might have guessed. To illustrate this little device one may sing a word beginning with *că*. While holding the vowel, each member of the group imagines the word which he thinks is being sung. Then the word is finished. *Cat, can, cab, cad, cap, cast,* and *calf* are all possibilities. Such devices may convince the students of the importance of final consonants and help overcome the inertia in pronouncing them.

4. *Diphthongs*

Do not think of *diphthongs* as being two vowels. Treat the shorter vowel as though it were a consonant so that the tone is sustained on one vowel and the quality is not changed throughout the duration of the tone. By this treatment the word *may* does not sound, *may - ee-,* but approaches, *meh - ee;* the word *new* does not become, *nee - oo -,* but sounds, *neoo -.* Do not treat the vowel *i (eye)* as the diphthong, *ah - ee;* pronounce it as *eye* and treat the closing *ee* as a consonant. How often have we heard, *America, the Beautiful* sung, "O, bee - you - ti - ful", or *The Star-Spangled Banner* sung, *"Oh - oo, say - ee - can you see!"*

Diction depends upon the free and unimpeded action of the articulators. They include a free jaw, flexible lips, and a loose tongue. Vowels should be practiced on sustained exercises and chords of songs until there is a blend throughout the various sections of the chorus on each vowel. Initial and final consonants may be practiced by selecting words from songs which utilize different vowels and then by repeating the words in rhythm on the pitches of comfortable descending scales. In this practice care must be taken that the accompanying consonants do not distort the vowel sound or a singing legato will be destroyed. Often such small words as *a, the, and, come,* and *love* are the most guilty in destroying a singing line. The teacher should demonstrate the rhythm to be used in the exercise to be sung by the group.

The following two examples illustrate the latter suggestion:

1. If the chorus is studying a fast madrigal or ballet, they may need to give some attention to the *fa, la, las.* In the following exercises, which all parts will sing in unison, errors in diction can be pointed out and corrected.

Fa, la, la, la, la,   Fa, la, la, la, la,   Fa, la, la, la, la,

Use the descending scale.
Sing in different scales and instruct high and low voices to join in when it is comfortable.
Phonetically the exercise should sound, *fah, lah, lah, lah, lah,* not *fah, luh, luh, luh, luh.*
La should be pronounced with the tip of the tongue without jaw movement.

2. This exercise can be adapted to any word of any song which seems to cause trouble. The rhythm of the word will suggest the rhythm of the exercise.

A - mer - i - ca, A - mer - i- ca, A - mer - i - ca,

Follow the suggestions given in the preceding exercise.
Phonetically the exercise should sound, *ah - mehr - i - cah,* not *uh - mayr - ee - cuh.*
Practice the last syllable alone if the *cah* causes any difficulty in pronouncing the consonant *k* without interfering with the vowel form.
Practice other words in the same manner.

Technical Accuracy

Much of the rehearsal time in the early stages of learning a new piece of music will be devoted to getting the rhythm and pitches worked out. This work can be done quickly if the conductor is thoroughly familiar with each part and can spot errors as soon as they appear. It is, of course, impossible to work on any refinements while the singers are still groping for pitches and singing the rhythm sluggishly.

When one section holds up the entire ensemble because it cannot grasp the technical difficulties, a separate sectional rehearsal will save time. It is difficult to hold the interest of other members of an ensemble if too much time is continually devoted to one section during rehearsals.

Ensemble

The ability to make perfect attacks and releases and to keep all parts together when making tempo changes is the result of using the eyes and ears. Members of an ensemble must understand the signals used by the conductor. If the conductor has a clear technic, the ensemble will soon learn to follow him perfectly. Specific attention should be given to acquiring perfect attacks and releases. Ensembles like to play the game of "follow the conductor" in which he varies tempos and introduces effects not written in the music in order to test the alertness of the group.

There is no substitute for alert listening in any music work. In group work this is particularly important if the ensemble is to function as a unit. It cannot be emphasized too strongly that a great deal of singing should be done without the aid of the conductor, depending entirely on the ear for keeping together. An ensemble that cannot do this is not likely to sing together even with the conductor on the podium.

INTERPRETATION

Some of the elements of interpretation have been discussed in Chapter Two. If the conductor is skillful enough to create an ensemble which has good tone quality, intonation, balance and blend, diction, and ensemble he will have a perfect technical instrument but nothing more. This technical instrument must now be made to live and this requires that the conductor be an artist. It is very doubtful whether any further directions than those already given will be of any great use because, if the conductor is a musician he will not need them; if he is not, no amount of written suggestions will be of any avail.

Problems and Procedures

1. Give some of your own ideas and exercises for the development of good tone quality.

2. Would you use special exercises or excerpts from music being studied when working on the various elements listed? Give specific illustrations of how you would proceed.

3. In your observation of high school groups, what one defect in choral singing have you found to be most outstanding? Can you offer an explanation for this?

4. Make a list of choral numbers which would meet the requirements laid down under *Tone Quality*.

5. Consider the advisability of using a reed organ rather than a piano when working with choral groups. Which would you prefer and why?

6. Attend a choral concert or song recital or listen to one over the radio and write down the words of two or three songs as they are sung. Do not guess at what is intended; write down actual sounds. Analyze them and form some conclusions as to the predominant errors.

Suggestions for Further Study

Cain, N. *Choral Music and Its Practice,* M. Witmark & Sons, 1932, Chap. X, XI, XII.

Christy, Van A. *Glee Club and Chorus,* G. Schirmer, Inc., 1940, Chap. IV.

Coward, H. *Choral Technique and Interpretation,* Novello & Co., Ltd., London, pp. 19-202, 249-278.

Dann, Hollis. *Hollis Dann Song Series, Conductor's Book,* American Book Company, 1936, pp. 8-35, 68-71, 107-109.

Davison, A. T. *Choral Conducting,* The Harvard University Press, 1940. This entire book should be carefully studied with special emphasis on Chap. V.

Evanson, J. " 'Pieces' or 'Fundamentals'—or Both", *Music Educators Journal,* Vol. XXIII, No. 2 (Oct., 1936), p. 24.

Finn, Wm. J. *The Art of the Choral Conductor,* C. C. Birchard & Company, 1939. The ambitious conductor will want to study the entire book.

Greene, H. P. *Interpretation in Song,* The Macmillan Company, Ltd., London, 1931, Parts I, II, III, IV, VI, Appendix.

Osburn, R. Lee. "Ensemble Singing in the Senior High School", *Music Educators Journal,* Vol. XVI, No. 2 (Dec., 1929), p. 53.

Pitts, C. M. *Pitts Voice Class Method,* Neil A. Kjos Music Company, 1936. The whole book pertains to problems mentioned in this chapter and offers invaluable suggestions.

Smallman and Wilcox. *The Art of A Cappella Singing,* Oliver Ditson Company, Inc., 1933.

Wilson, H. R. *Music in the High School,* Silver Burdett Company, Chap. VI, VII.

Wilson, H. R. *The Solo Singer,* Carl Fischer, Inc., 1941. Useful vocalises in obtaining correct tone production.

Wodell, F. W. *Choir and Chorus Conducting,* Theodore Presser Co., 1931.

Young, T. Campbell. " 'Vocal Diction'—in a Nutshell", *Music Educators Journal,* Vol. XIX, No. 1 (Oct., 1932).

CHAPTER SEVEN

THE INSTRUMENTAL REHEARSAL

The conductor of an instrumental ensemble faces a much more complex situation than does the conductor of a choral ensemble. In the choral ensemble there is only one instrument, the voice, and thus only one set of principles for correct usage are needed. In the instrumental ensemble, however, each instrument has its own peculiar set of principles and the conductor must have some knowledge of correct teaching technics for each instrument.

Once again it should be emphasized that an ensemble is a group of individuals and that it is the ability of the individual which determines the strength of an ensemble. The finest conductor alive cannot make a good ensemble out of a group composed of players with an incorrect foundation in the playing of their instruments. It is good teaching which makes possible a good ensemble. The ground work laid before the player enters an advanced ensemble should be extensive and thorough.

The ensemble which is fed by players taught by competent teachers is indeed fortunate but this does not relieve the conductor of the responsibility of being familiar with correct teaching procedures for each instrument. He must be able to detect immediately any imperfections and to offer remedies. Players who know better, will often do things in group playing which they would never attempt to do in solo playing. When inaccuracies of this sort are not checked immediately, the player may grow careless, knowing he can get away with them. And since all those who teach are not necessarily competent, the conductor must be prepared to make changes in any player's technic in order to put him on the right path.

One of the serious obstacles to obtaining good musical results from a school band has been the recent emphasis placed on the early development of a marching unit. The primary reason for any musical ensemble existing in any educational system is to give training in musical performance, an idea emphasized by Hindsley:

> "Since, then, the raison-d' etre of a band is music, it seems reasonable that band training should be dominated by the musical idea, with the marching relegated to its proper place as quite an important element. The very first thing a band should do is lay a foundation for future good playing. When it can play march music with some degree of proficiency, it should learn to march. From then on the marching ability may be developed as rapidly as possible, so long as it does not seriously interfere with reasonable progress in playing."[1]

---

[1] M. Hindsley, "The Marching Band", *Music Educators Journal,* Vol. XVII, No. 2 (December, 1930).

It is not the purpose of this chapter to go into the teaching technics of each instrument. Such knowledge can best be obtained from competent instructors, as can a knowledge of correct voice production principles. The aim here is to make such suggestions as can be used in the rehearsal to enable the instrumental ensemble to realize in varying degrees the aims set up in Chapter Five.

TONE QUALITY

In choral music, the sustained tone was held to be the basis of good singing. In instrumental music, the sustained, singing tone is likewise the foundation for all good playing. In support of this idea, hear what Richard Wagner has to say:

> "Players of stringed instruments should copy the full-toned piano of the best winds, and the latter, again, should endeavor to imitate the best vocalists.
> "The sustained soft tone here spoken of, and the sustained powerful tone mentioned above, are the two poles of orchestral expression."[1]

An ensemble which has as its goal the ability to play a sustained tone and reaches this goal will have accomplished something to be proud of and will have laid the foundation for some fine playing. School groups, both bands and orchestras, are particularly weak in this respect, a weakness which is not so apparent in rapidly moving passages but which shows up woefully in slow, sustained passages. Edwin Franko Goldman who has heard hundreds of school bands in his capacity as a contest adjudicator and guest conductor, writes:

> "My experience has proved that the prime test for any band is the playing of a slow movement. At many contest and music festivals which I have attended, one band after another would appear and open its program with a march, then an overture or other standard or classic work. In the playing of the marches, it is more difficult to judge the actual quality of a band because of the spirited tempo, and because so many of the minor parts are generally concealed, often covered up by the drums. The overture may start with a lively tempo, but as soon as the slow tempo is reached, the bottom seems to fall out of the band, and it is then that one discovers the real weaknesses—the poor tonal quality and the very bad intonation. It is in these slow movements that one can see whether the individual players actually have the command and control of an instrument. Good tone and good intonation are the prime assets of fine wind instrument playing."[2]

---

[1] R. Wagner, *On Conducting*, William Reeves, London, 1919, p. 33.
[2] E. F. Goldman, *Band Betterment*, Carl Fischer, Inc., 1934, p. 82.

A good instrumental tone is free, resonant, and expressive, corresponding in these respects to a good vocal tone. The conductor must have a thorough conception of the accepted tonal quality of each musical instrument and he must know how good a quality of tone high school players can be expected to develop. Normally, not enough is expected from a high school player and the result is achievement below that which could have been attained. The conductor who is tone conscious will soon make members of the ensemble just as conscious of it and an important step along the way will have been taken.

Here are some factors which should receive consideration in the work on tone:

(1.) *The condition and quality of the equipment used* is the first consideration in the production of tone. The tone quality of a stringed instrument may be affected by a sound-post out of position, a bridge improperly placed or too thick and clumsy, poor strings, insufficient hair in the bow, or a bow filled with old hair saturated with rosin. Strings and, likewise, all instruments in the ensemble, should be carefully checked to see that they are in condition to work at their maximum efficiency.

An ensemble using the cheapest instruments made cannot be expected to get as good tonal quality as it would with better equipment. This applies also to the percussion group. Cymbals in particular must have a ringing tone quality. A good pair should be added to the ensemble with part of the first funds available.

Wind-instrument players are more fortunate than string players because they can, at small cost, purchase an additional piece of equipment which may materially improve tone quality as well as all-round performance. That piece of equipment is a good mouthpiece. Nothing can make a poor instrument into a good one, but a mouthpiece can make an improvement. In order then, to improve tone quality as well as other elements of playing, a wind-instrument player should be equipped with a good mouthpiece, selected to fit the individual.

Reeds can be classified as equipment. The selection of proper reeds is so important that it cannot be mentioned too often. Players must learn to be very critical in their selection of reeds and must learn to make what alterations may be necessary in order to produce a good tone. Some conductors have a weekly reed inspection and anyone playing on an inferior reed is not permitted to play until he has a good one. Reeds are an expense and thus create a problem, but the conductor must solve it if best results are to be obtained.

(2.) *Breath management for wind players* is just as important as it is for singers. The principles of correct breathing, discussed in Chapter Six, are also applicable for the wind player. He, too, must learn to breathe deeply with the corresponding action around the waist line without a collapsing of the chest position. As in singing, the wind player should breathe through the mouth when playing. Ability to breathe in this manner assures better coordinated action in playing an instrument. A round, beautiful tone is dependent upon this free, coordinated action and the transfer of much of the work of playing to the large breathing muscles.

The expiration of the breath in playing a wind instrument is, likewise, similar to that in singing. There is a feeling of resting down on the breath, not a feeling of pulling up or straining. There is not a conscious holding back of the breath but a continuous breathing into the tone. For wind players the adage, "Sing with the breath" becomes, "Play with the breath". The phrase "Breathe into the tone" applies equally to playing a wind instrument and singing. Breath control in playing a wind instrument is obtained by establishing a balance of breath between the resistance offered by the vibrating embouchure or reed and the continued expiration of the breath. The embouchure or reed in playing have the same function as the vocal cords in singing. Without a correct and developed embouchure, proper breath management in playing a wind instrument is not possible.

3. *Correct embouchure development* for wind-instrument players is essential if good tone quality is to be obtained. If this is not accomplished, all other elements may be carried out perfectly and still the desired results not obtained.

It is not advisable to give general suggestions for the development of embouchure. Each instrument has individual problems of embouchure development with which the conductor must be acquainted.

4. *Playing with as full a tone as the player is capable of producing* should be a part of daily practice. String players must practice with vigorous, full strokes of the bows; wind-instrument players must play with just as much vigor. Tonal brilliance cannot be developed through continued soft playing, important as such playing is. This loud practicing, controlled, of course, should be done individually rather than in the large ensemble, since such playing in the ensemble would induce poor balance and other faults.

5. *To practice sustained tones,* it is generally agreed, is the best method of developing tone quality and tone control. First there should be practice on an even dynamic level, then with a long crescendo followed by a long diminuendo. This practice is just as valuable for string players as it is for wind players, because it develops a firm, steady bow which is to tone control on a stringed instrument what good breath control is to the wind-instrument player.

Playing long tones is very boring and only the most conscientious player will do enough of it to obtain any value from it. For school groups it is often better to play music of a sustained type or music which contains long slurs and so demands continuous, steady tone production. This leads to bow control and embouchure development. Bach Chorales are especially valuable for such practice, but conductors should not feel that they are a panacea for all ills.

6. *Tonal development should precede tongue, finger, and bow dexterity.* One of the best ways to arrest tonal development is to be continually playing marches and overtures in which the primary attention must be given to note chasing. If a sustained tone is to be the basis of all good playing, then sustained music should be used a great deal of the time. The insistence on early development of speedy tonguing is particularly harmful to wind-instrument players. Slurred passages which require only a moderate amount of finger technic, but demand a steady flow of tone, are safer to use.

7. *Imitation plays a very important part in tonal development.* A good example of fine tone should be heard as often as possible. If one student possesses a good tone, the others should be encouraged to imitate him.

8. *There should be some natural aptitude for the instrument the student chooses.* A student may attempt to play an instrument for which he has little or no talent. This person may find that he is able to produce a much more musical tone on some other kind of instrument. Good tone is an indication of a mature player, but even from the very first lessons there are limits to the amount of poor tone quality which a player may be expected to produce. The school music conductor must assume some responsibility in guiding students in the selection of instruments. This responsibility can be discharged only if the conductor has a thorough working knowledge of every instrument in the orchestra and band and is familiar with studies made on this subject.

INTONATION

Very often the outstanding characteristic of an amateur musical group, school groups included, is the complete abandon with which they play out of tune. Perfect intonation is seldom possible with a high school instrumental group but good intonation is quite possible and very poor intonation, the kind so often heard, is hard to excuse. Certainly no one element of good musical performance will so thoroughly engage the attention of the conductor. It is quite likely that a major part of many rehearsals will be spent on it and certainly some part of every rehearsal will be devoted to it.

Anyone with a musical ear will be immediately conscious of out-of-tune playing. Many high school players have good ears and realize that something is wrong but do very little about it until the conductor demands a correction. Others do not hear as keenly but will notice it after it has been called to their attention. The first problem here is, as it was in tonal development, to establish a consciousness of the problem of intonation. The major burden for this will rest on the conductor's shoulders but the better players will help out considerably once standards of what is expected have been established.

The factors listed below play an important part in the development of good intonation in instrumental groups:

1. *Tonal development and good intonation go hand in hand in many respects.* A tone that is controlled, resting on good breath support and embouchure development is, in the case of wind-instrument players, very likely to be fairly well in tune or under control enough to make good intonation possible. In the same way, the condition of the instrument affects both tone and intonation.

Humoring the tone, so necessary in all wind-instrument playing, can only be done when a certain amount of control exists. Humoring the tone too early in the playing career may deter proper embouchure development since it may result in a shifting position of the embouchure.

2. *Some passages may be fingered in several different ways.* As a general rule, one of these fingerings will be better in tune than the others and should be used, particularly in sustained passages. The trombonist will find that D above the staff is better in tune when played in fourth position than when played in first position. Each wind instrument has its own peculiarities and good intonation is possible only when the player is thoroughly aware of all possible ways of playing and altering each tone.

The string players must have a thorough knowledge of all positions. Many passages will be played badly out of tune because too many shifts are being made and in other instances because shifts are not being made. Intonation in each position presents a separate problem since the spaces between tones are not the same in any two positions.

3. *There should be a standard pitch to which the ensemble is tuned.* The use of the oboe is often a mistake because in the hands of an amateur player, this instrument is capable of pitch variations. The equipment of an instrumental rehearsal room should include a tuning bar which will sound an A (440) for orchestra and a B♭ for band.

String players who tune to a low-pitched piano at home often find that their instruments will not stay in tune when tuned to the pitch of A (440).

The string players who do not carefully tune their instruments many times each day will find that the instruments will not hold a set pitch.

4. *The whole instrument must be tuned.* The idea of having a tuning note for band and orchestra has unfortunately led to the idea that this is the only tone which needs tuning. This misconception leads to much out-of-tune playing.

One of the best ways to tune the entire instrument is to have the ensemble play a few unison scales. A small reed organ, carefully tuned, can be used to give the correct pitch of each tone. The value of having such an organ is that players can practice with it and have a standard for comparison.

5. *String- and wind-instrument players should sing.* Passages which cause trouble may be sung slowly and then played. The value of this procedure cannot be over-emphasized. When singing, each tone must be sensed before it can be voiced. In playing any instrument this must be done if good intonation is to be obtained. The practice of playing a tone in order to hear what it sounds like should be discouraged. Singing is one of the best ways of developing pitch anticipation.

6. *Intonation is the string player's greatest problem* and it is difficult to give many suggestions for attaining it except to listen and practice. All string players, however, must have a thorough grasp of where whole and half-steps occur. Violinists in particular, often play "between the cracks" because their fingers are not in position to play either a half-step or a whole-step.

7. *The type of music* which is favorable to good tonal development is also favorable to the development of intonation. Slow, sustained music gives the ear a chance to analyze intonation and dictate adjustments. Slow music is not harder to play in tune than fast music, it is just that intonation deficiencies are more easily heard. In fast music the notes are played so rapidly that bad intonation is not as obvious when it exists. If this statement is doubted, play a six-eight march in regular tempo and then play it with six slow beats to a measure.

8. *A considerable amount of soft playing is essential* to the development of good intonation. In soft playing, no forcing occurs and the ear is able to hear defects and remedy them. Much loud playing induces forcing and results in poor intonation. Marches which utilize extreme ranges and extreme dynamics are detrimental unless used in moderation.

9. *Tuning must be continued all the time.* Unison scales can be used to good advantage in the improvement of intonation. However, playing a

few unison scales and then forgetting intonation during the remainder of the rehearsal will have no worthwhile effect.

The emphasis must be not alone on playing the instrument in tune but on playing in tune together. This implies concessions on the part of all players, some humoring the tone up and the others coming down to meet them. Particularly good passages for intonation work will be found in any piece where unisons, octaves, or perfect fifths exist, as these are the easiest intervals to tune. Each section can first be tuned in this manner and then one section at a time added, making necessary alterations along the line until the entire ensemble is playing.

(10.) *Vibrato must not be used* when string players are trying to clean up the intonation. Good intonation depends on exact placing of the fingers and vibrato often covers up faulty finger placement.

(11.) *Eliminate temporarily the players who have the greatest difficulty with intonation.* As their intonation improves, they may rejoin the ensemble. It is unfair to the majority of the students to have their work spoiled by a small minority of the group. One player can spoil the intonation of an entire section.

(12.) *Correct intonation on high tones* offers considerable difficulty to many wind-instrument players. Good intonation is more easily obtainable if fewer players are placed on the upper parts. The general practice is to place too many players on the upper parts, resulting in lack of balance as well as in poor intonation, since upper tones are more audible than lower tones.

(13.) *The temperature of the room* has a great deal to do with intonation. Unusually high or low temperatures affect all instruments in varying degrees and will spoil the intonation of an ensemble which under normal conditions might be good.

BALANCE AND BLEND

High school ensembles are usually made up of poor, average, and good players. From such a mixture the conductor must obtain a certain degree of balance if worthwhile musical effects are to be realized. It is, of course, much easier to develop a balanced ensemble when the proficiency of the players is not so varied. Consequently, one of the first steps in organization for the teacher is to develop instrumental classes and different grades of ensembles. The beginning ensembles will provide players for the more advanced groups. The ensemble which contains students who have played for a number of years and some who are beginners will find it difficult to attain balance. When an ensemble is composed of both beginning and advanced players and it does not seem advisable to the teacher to separate them, he must secure music which is especially arranged for such groups. Publishers are providing more and more of this type of music.

Another problem in organization which must be considered before good balance can be obtained is the matter of instrumentation. All instrumental groups should be aiming towards achieving an instrumentation which will make satisfactory results possible. This does not mean that a large ensemble of symphonic proportions is necessary but it does mean that whatever the size of the group is, it should contain the essential instruments and they should be in proper proportion to each other. An orchestra with a large wind section and a small string section, or a band with a large brass section and small woodwind section cannot be made to sound well balanced.

Even when all players in an ensemble are capable of playing the same music and when a good instrumentation is maintained, balance will not necessarily result. In the rehearsal itself the following points may be given attention:

1. In the discussion on tone and intonation it has been pointed out that arousing the ensemble to a consciousness of what is wanted is of paramount importance. Balance is the first requisite of ensemble playing and calls for keen listening. A player must know the relative importance of his part; he must know where the melody lies in every measure. An ensemble player has as much to think about as a soloist; he is a member of a team and poor judgment on his part may spoil the efforts of the remainder of the ensemble.

It takes time to learn all these things. The player will soon find that tones which he thinks are too loud, too soft, or just right do not sound the same to the conductor. If the conductor keeps making suggestions, the player will soon learn just how much tone is needed in order to give his part the importance it deserves.

2. Divide the good players among all the parts. It is a mistake to put all the poor players on the lower parts, such as second violin, or second and third trumpet and clarinet. Following this policy is one of the surest ways not to get balance. Balance depends on an equal distribution of strength on all parts, or possibly having just a little more strength on the lower parts than on the upper ones. Of course, every solo part must have a strong leader but so should every lower part. Of the six best violinists in an orchestra two at least should play second violin. The four best cornetists in a band might well be assigned to lead each of the four parts. Of course, the technical ability of the player and demands of the part must be given consideration. There are many instances where a violinist does not have enough command of the positions to play first violin but has a fine sense

of rhythm and will make an excellent leader of the second violin section.

(3.) It has already been suggested in the discussion of tone that more players should be assigned to the lower parts than to the upper parts. This will also lead to better balance. The approved string instrumentation calls for two more first violins than second violins. This is, however, based on the assumption that all players have somewhat the same proficiency which is true of professional groups. In school work, this ratio may be reversed with good results.

In the band, a trombone section of six players will usually be divided into two firsts, two seconds and two thirds. This will work out quite well if the three best players are each leading a part. It is not inconceivable, however, that a distribution of one first, two seconds, and three thirds would at times result in better balance.

(4.) In the orchestra, the string tone is meant to predominate most of the time. In the band the same is true of the woodwinds. Ensembles which do not bring about this result will not achieve proper balance.

It is assumed here that the symphonic band, with its greater musical potentialities, has been set up as the ideal rather than the military brass band. It is quite natural that during the transition period, most bands will continue to give undue prominence to the brass and percussion sections. The refinement added to a band when woodwinds outnumber the brasses is entirely obliterated when the brass and percussion play without regard for their more delicately toned friends. The brass and percussion players may never use all of their power while the woodwinds have an important part. In pure brass passages, more power may be utilized.

(5.) The first step in obtaining balance is to develop it within each section. A well balanced section will sound like one instrument. Some of the better players often will cause trouble since their tones are powerful and they have not learned to listen carefully.

After each section is balanced within itself, various sections can be put together. 'Cellos and string basses playing in octaves as they so often do, must play balanced octaves. When French horns and trombones are playing the same part, the trombones must not predominate. They must blend in with the horns.

(6.) There is always at least one player whose tone is of such quality that when used with the same power as the others in his section, it will stand out. In order to obtain blend from this type of player it is necessary to have him play lighter than his partners at all times. In the meantime, the conductor must try to eliminate the reasons for the faulty tone and, failing in this, suggest a change to another instrument.

Technical Accuracy

Acquiring a technically correct performance from an instrumental group requires that the conductor have a thorough grasp of the score. Each of the separate parts must be studied and checked for accuracy at each rehearsal. It is a mistake to spend so much time on the lead parts that other parts are neglected, but this very mistake is often committed by the inexperienced conductor.

Hearing technical errors and placing the blame where it belongs requires a keen ear and experience with an instrumental group. There are certain tones on each instrument which are a little awkward to play and when a wrong tone is heard near such a tone, it will usually be found to be the awkward tone which was missed. Examples of such tones in brass music are found in keys where open tones cannot be used and in string music in keys where open strings cannot be used. The tone color peculiar to each instrument is another help in spotting the player who made the error.

There are certain passages on all instruments which must be played by employing unusual fingerings. This is particularly true of the strings and woodwinds and if correct technical accuracy is to be obtained, the conductor must be familiar with such fingerings.

String music presents a special problem because it requires a knowledge of the various bowings in order to play it correctly. In fact the whole string technic is so complicated that special string training of an extensive nature is a requirement for the orchestral conductor unless he has a string teacher to help him.

The best way of obtaining correct technical accuracy is to hold special sectional rehearsals where all of the conductor's attention can be centered on a smaller number of parts and players.

Ensemble

The suggestions given in the discussion of the choral rehearsal in Chapter Six apply here. Good ensemble is more difficult to obtain from an instrumental group than it is from a choral group and as a result it will require more time to achieve it.

A helpful procedure is to have the players put down their instruments and count as the conductor beats, watching intently the particular measures in which the faulty playing occurs. This procedure enables the group to feel the ritard or accelerando and makes the playing itself easier. It is only when the entire ensemble feels each phrase in the same manner that a large group will play together perfectly.

Instrumental ensembles have a special seating problem. The first rule a player should learn in ensemble work is that he must sit where he can see the music and the conductor at the same time. The conductor must check carefully to see that this is done.

Rushing is one of the worst foes of good ensemble playing and it is indulged in freely by high school groups. This fault is a result of excitement and careless treatment of rhythmic values. Ensemble players must be particularly well grounded in the rhythmic element of music for it is rhythm which holds a group together. Many successful instrumental conductors develop a good rhythmic foundation through the use of foot-beating while others use vocal counting. The method is not so important as long as it results in exact playing of all common rhythmic figures. Without this ability no instrumental group can perform as a unit.

INTERPRETATION

The instrumental conductor must be just as careful of phrasing as is the choral conductor. There are no words to help determine phrase endings and *nuances but they are there and must be found. The phrase in instrumental music should be sung just as it is in vocal music, something that is not always done. The conductor must be able to indicate phrase nuance with his baton technic.

A good interpreter shows restraint; he does not attempt something for which his technical capabilities are not equal. The peak of a climax will not be musical if it calls for so much power that noise rather than musical sound is the result. The high school instrumental conductor will be expected to measure the capabilities of his ensemble intelligently and secure as inspiring an interpretation as their capabilities will permit. The wise conductor will not "wear out" emotionally the members of the ensemble during rehearsals, but he will reserve the emotional peak for the concert.

* Nuance — a slight or delicate variation in tone, color, meaning, etc.; shade of difference.

PROBLEMS AND PROCEDURES

1. Write a list of suggestions for improving tone quality on the instrument you know best. Test your knowledge of the string, brass, and woodwind families by doing the same for one member of each family.

2. Make a similar list of suggestions for improving intonation.

3. In your experience, which section of the high school orchestra is usually the weakest? Which of the band? How do you account for these weaknesses?

4. Pick out six band or orchestral numbers which are conducive to improvement of tone and intonation. Find a few which you would consider to be detrimental.

5. Make up a balanced instrumentation for a 30 piece band or orchestra, also for a 40 and 50 piece group.

6. Explain the procedures you would use in teaching rhythm.

SUGGESTIONS FOR FURTHER STUDY

GOLDMAN, E. F. *Band Betterment,* Carl Fischer, Inc., 1934, Chap. X, XV, XVII, XIX, XXX, XXXI, XXXII.

HINDSLEY, M. H. "The Instrumental Music Teacher", *Music Educators Journal,* Vol. XXIV, No. 3 (Dec., 1937), p. 34.

LAMP, C. H. "Can Aptitude for Specific Musical Instruments Be Determined?", *1936 Yearbook,* Music Educators National Conference, p. 246.

MADDY and GIDDINGS. *Instrumental Technique,* The Willis Music Co., 1926, Chap. VI, VII, VIII, XII, XV, XVI.

NORMAN, T. F. *Instrumental Music in the Public Schools,* Theodore Presser Co., 1940, Chap. IX.

VAN BODEGRAVEN, P. *Organizing a School Band,* Long Island City, New York: Penzel, Mueller and Co., 1938, pp. 26-30, 33-42, 50-56.

WILSON, H. R. *Music in the High School,* Silver Burdett Company, 1941, Chap. IX.

Recalcitrant — refusing to obey authority, custom, regulation, etc.; stubbornly defiant.

CHAPTER EIGHT

REHEARSAL PROCEDURES

It is quite possible for a person to be a good musician, to understand the musical requirements of good ensemble performance, to know how to fulfill these requirements, and still not be a successful conductor. There are· many non-musical essentials of rehearsal procedure which must be recognized and applied in order to lay the groundwork for obtaining the best musical results. This is particularly true when working with high school students. An understanding of the high school student as an individual is just as essential, if not more essential than an understanding of the music being studied. Let us examine now, some of the more important non-musical essentials of an ensemble rehearsal.

DISCIPLINE

Any serious mental work requires concentration, and concentration in a large group requires discipline. In educational work discipline should not be considered as imposed authority but rather, self-control through the desire to cooperate. The conductor who is not able to obtain self-controlled discipline from his group will hardly be able to do a superior quality of musical work. The ensemble in which everyone is busy producing music which they enjoy will have the true basis for maintaining discipline. When the conductor steps upon the podium he should expect and insist upon whole-hearted attention. He will secure this type of attention by knowing his business and making rehearsals interesting with his enthusiasm for music and young people.

On the other hand, the school music conductor is also a teacher and he will continuously be walking among the players offering suggestions and giving help. When discipline problems arise he will quietly, but firmly, point out to both individuals and ensembles the need for cooperation in any group effort. Students who cannot cooperate in making music together with other students should not have the privilege of playing with a group. Recalcitrants are better off in activities in which they are more interested and in which they are willing to cooperate. Little actions which do not directly or indirectly affect the efficiency of the rehearsal need not be considered a breach of discipline. In other words, the conductor is dealing with red-blooded, energetic, young people and he cannot expect the impossible.

Discipline in music ensembles can best be attained through keeping students busy, knowing your business, and creating interest by your own interest in and enthusiasm for the music that is being studied and performed. This statement presupposes music worthy of such interest and enthusiasm. Self-controlled discipline and cooperation is one of the most valuable lessons that students can learn in ensemble performance. The conductor, who is an educator, will capitalize on the situation that music organizations offer for such training.

REHEARSAL PLANS

Prescott and Chidester[1] advise that the band rehearsal be divided into three parts, devoting 5 to 15 minutes to ensemble drill, 30 to 50 minutes to concert preparation, and 3 to 5 minutes to recreation and motivation. Each conductor will have his own ideas as to the division of time but it is important that some plan be adopted and followed. The plan should not be the same for each rehearsal, for this would be deadening to interest.

A long range plan of attack on each number being rehearsed is also advisable. If a plan book is kept, it is easy to see the stage of development of each number. The method of rehearsing each number will be determined by the previous study given to it. Henry Coward[2] lists three methods of rehearsal: The Conventional Generalizing; The Critical Particularizing; and The Compartmental Specializing.

The Conventional Generalizing Method is used with new numbers. The plan is to go over the entire number several times to become acquainted with the general spirit and idea. No attempt is made in this rehearsal to stop for corrections. This might be considered the "whole" method of learning as opposed to the "part" method and is supported by the most recent psychological findings.

It is useless during early rehearsals of a number to be continually stopping because of wrong notes or other mechanical errors. Many of these errors are due to lack of control and the performer will eliminate them on his own initiative if given an opportunity to do so. There is, of course, a danger in the over-use of this method. If continued too long, faults will become habits and will not be easily eliminated.

The Particularizing Method consists in striving for perfection in all details of musical performance. This method will follow the use of the Conventional Generalizing Method and presupposes that the student has

[1] Prescott and Chidester, *Getting Results with School Bands*, Paul A. Schmitt Music Company and Carl Fischer, Inc., 1938, p. 100.
[2] H. Coward, *Choral Technique and Interpretation*, Novello & Co., Ltd., London, p. 9.

been given time to make the corrections of which he is capable. This type
of rehearsal requires many interruptions to make corrections. Because
of these many interruptions, this method can easily become very tiresome
to the students and should be used only during part of the rehearsal period.
However, the ability to "polish" a number in this manner is necessary if
the work of the ensemble is to be lifted out of the commonplace. The ability
to concentrate on small details has often been called one characteristic
of a genius.

The Compartmental Specializing Method consists in concentrating all
attention on one special point to the exclusion of everything else. The
special point might be diction in which case all other mistakes would be
ignored. Such a method of rehearsing would be used only when the
ensemble seemed particularly slow in achieving the desired results in some
specific phase of musical performance such as tone or intonation. It serves
to make the ensemble keenly aware of their shortcomings. This method
should not be used for every rehearsal, but only occasionally when concentration is needed on one phase of work.

A good rehearsal plan will certainly call for the use of the first two
methods of procedure. This combination of methods will make for variety
as well as systematic progress. No plan must become so rigid that it cannot
be varied. The plan for each rehearsal must of necessity be partially based
on the results of the previous one. The conductor will notice errors, all of
which cannot be corrected at once, and will check the sections of the score
in which the errors fall so that they can be remedied in the following
rehearsal.

WARMING UP

Playing or singing requires mental and physical coordination. In preparing to participate in an ensemble rehearsal, an individual must warm
up his instrument and concentrate his attention on the job to be done. The
necessity of mental preparation is not often stressed but the lack of it may
nullify correct physical preparations. We suggest three ways of warming
up for ensemble participation:

(1.) Warm up the ensemble by performing a piece of music. This offers
the advantage of using every spare moment of the rehearsal period in work
on actual concert material. The practice of using a march to warm up a
band is not recommended because it stresses fast, loud playing, quite the
opposite of what is needed for opening material. It is safe to say that when
an actual piece of music is used for warming up, it should have a medium
range, a slow tempo, sustained notes for all performers, and no extremes
in dynamics. Again we suggest Bach Chorales or hymns as excellent
material for "warming up" both choral and instrumental groups.

②. Warming up may be made an individual responsibility so that actual work on concert material can be started as soon as the conductor steps on the podium. Certainly every musician should know how to "warm up" and should be able to take this responsibility on himself. Nevertheless, intelligent use of warming up procedures by high school performers is not common. The usual result is that, when left to their own devices, the singers do nothing or shout, the trumpet players pick up their instruments and try to blow their top note while the reed and string players show equal thoughtlessness. Therefore, if warming up is made an individual responsibility, the conductor will find it necessary to be on hand to see that it is done intelligently and suggest proper procedures for each instrument.

③. Playing or singing before the rehearsal may be entirely prohibited and all warming up done in the ensemble, using exercises especially written for the purpose. Unison scales and sustained chords are among the best of these for instrumental groups while the vocal ensembles may use vocalises which give special attention to developing freedom and flexibility.[1]

Each of the above methods of warming up is used by successful high school musical groups and it would not be advisable to try to prove one superior to the other. The conductor must experiment with each method to see which best suits the ensemble under his direction. A change of procedure might be the answer. By all means do not use the same set of exercises for warming up. Vary this procedure by using sustained music at the beginning of rehearsal periods. What obtains best results with one group will not always do so with another; but whatever method is used, close attention to the job at hand must be demanded. The warming up period is used to gain control of tone and intonation, and to loosen muscles of the tongue, fingers, and arm. All of these things require the keenest of mental effort which should carry over into the preparation of numbers to be performed.

THE SECTIONAL REHEARSAL

The conductor who is able to schedule frequent separate rehearsals for each section of his ensemble is indeed fortunate. This might almost be called a necessity for fine performance. In a large ensemble, very little attention can be given each individual and only a little more to each section since both procedures require the remainder of the ensemble to be idle. Some attention to individuals and sections is necessary but when one particular section needs a great deal of attention, it is far more efficient to meet that section alone. It is often more advantageous to have two or

---

[1] H. R. Wilson, *The Solo Singer,* Carl Fischer, Inc., 1941. The exercises on flexibility are especially valuable for warming up.

three full ensemble rehearsals a week with sectional rehearsals the other days than to hold a full rehearsal daily but no sectionals.

The aims of the sectional rehearsal will be the same as those for the full rehearsal but much more specific work can be done since the individual is better able to hear what he is doing and receives more help from the conductor. The sectional rehearsal is especially valuable for working out difficult technical passages but the important items of tone, intonation, balance, and interpretation must always be in the foreground.

PSYCHOLOGICAL FACTORS

There is a certain amount of similarity between the procedures of a doctor and those of a teacher. A doctor will advise preventive practices which will keep the patient well but when trouble occurs he will diagnose the case and prescribe a remedy. The teacher, by using correct procedures, will attempt to keep the pupil from falling into bad habits but when difficulties are encountered the teacher will also diagnose the case, decide on the cause and then prescribe a remedy. But from here on the similarity disappears because the patient is usually forced to take a doctor's prescription while the teacher must awaken interest in the pupil so that he will make intelligent use of the prescription. This is just the reason why many musicians with a fine musical background fail as conductors of high school ensemble music. Here is where psychological factors enter. There are now two considerations: music and the student. A knowledge of both is essential. The subject is much too large to enter into thoroughly in a few pages but let us indicate three psychological factors which are of paramount importance in any group music work.

(1.) *Interest* is the chief factor in developing a will to learn. Without interest, learning is inefficient and ineffective.

The first job of the conductor must be then, to arouse interest. This means that rehearsals must be enjoyable; they must have serious moments and humorous moments; they must be inspiring and create enthusiasm. Above all, the music itself must be of such nature that it will hold the interest and attention of the group.

(2.) Proper *motivation* is needed to develop this will to learn. This motivation originates with the conductor and may take many original forms. Three sources of motivation which should receive consideration are:

(a) *The attitude of the conductor.* It is natural for a student to desire the approbation of the conductor. Approbation must, however, be used intelligently if it is to have any motivating force. Praise should be sincere and should be given only when the student has really achieved something.

Indiscriminate praise passed out freely on all occasions will hardly inspire a student to better performance. It may easily have the opposite effect.

(b) *The presence of a group.* The conductor who has worked as a private teacher often finds it difficult to capitalize on the psychological opportunities presented by the group and the natural desires set up by group work.

The desire to excel is very strong. This is particularly true in group work where it is easy to compare individual achievement. The system of tryouts used by so many instrumental groups, in which each person plays a selected passage and is seated according to the comparative proficiency with which he plays it, capitalizes this desire to excel. Whatever the method, superior work must be recognized in a tangible manner if the desire to excel is to be encouraged.

The desire to cooperate is natural to most students and can be used freely in group work. The student must be made to feel that he is working in a cooperative venture and that he is expected to make a real contribution to that venture, preferably by his musical accomplishments, although there are other ways in which he can be made to feel as though he is a cooperating member of a group. These include acting as librarian, stage manager, publicity director, or in any other capacity in which his efforts are making a distinct contribution to the welfare of the group. In contrast to the method of seating described in the preceding paragraph, many conductors are capitalizing upon the desire to cooperate by locating students in the ensemble regardless of their individual skill. This procedure should reap fine educational results.

The desire for group approval is a very powerful motivating factor which the conductor should use. The student who can sing or play his part well should be given an opportunity to do so alone so that he can obtain group approval for his efforts and inspire others to do likewise. Group disapproval is also a powerful factor and will often result in a desirable reaction from a certain type of student.

A different kind of group approval is that which makes public appearance such a powerful motivating factor. Here it is the approval of the audience which is sought, not for the individual, but for the entire ensemble. A student whose interest has been truly aroused will have a feeling of pride in the work of his organization, and also a sense of loyalty which will demand that he do his part in making the public appearance of his group a real success. Anyone who has directed a high school musical group will attest to the tremendous motivating power of a public appearance. The conductor must insist that the group do everything within its power to put on a performance which will obtain group approval from the audience. With this as its objective, any group will do better work. The one danger to guard against is making public appearances when not adequately prepared. After a few of these, the conductor will find the ensemble becoming accustomed to lower standards of performance and much of the motivation for better work inspired by the public appearance will be lost.

(c) A third psychological factor is the pride which comes from a sense of increasing mastery. In this connection, Mursell and Glenn say:

> "It has been conclusively shown that learners always do better if they have before them an objective record of their own progress. . . . In other types of school work this is one of the great arguments for frequent testing. In music, however, it is a good deal harder to apply the principle. Here we see the great danger of mere amiability on the part of the teacher. It is very important for her to take a positive and appreciative attitude, and to avoid scolding and fault finding. But it is quite equally important for her to remain effectively and wisely critical."[1]

And again:

> "That is to say, we want a positive tendency, a tendency to look for and appreciate good work, rather than a tendency to look for and blame poor work. Part of the art of teaching lies in taking this point of view without at the same time sacrificing standards, and relapsing into a totally uncritical geniality. When this tendency emerges, the value of a helpful attitude is eliminated, for then the pupils have no real idea whether they are doing well or badly, and the will to learn is lulled to sleep by indiscriminate praise. In general, we would suggest that the teacher should look for and appreciate effort and willingness rather than pay somewhat insincere compliments to a musical result which in and of itself may be rather mediocre."[2]

The conductor is responsible for seeing that each student is proceeding according to a plan which will result in increased mastery. This will obviously require that weak points be pointed out as well as strong points for it is only by recognizing weaknesses that they can be overcome. When a weakness is pointed out, a remedy must be suggested. Then as increasing mastery is developed, the conductor should comment on it as recognition of work well done. It is quite important also, that the increased ability be felt and recognized by the student himself and by other members of the ensemble. In such a situation we have the three motivating factors of approval of the conductor, approval of the group, and sense of increasing mastery all being utilized at the same time.

---

[1] Mursell and Glenn, *The Psychology of School Music Teaching,* Silver Burdett Company, 1938, p. 95.
[2] *Ibid.,* p. 93.

③ *Long practice periods are less effective than more numerous, shorter periods.*

This is an important psychological guide in scheduling rehearsals. Many instrumental groups and some vocal groups hold long, tiring rehearsals, the later part of which becomes a struggle between the conductor and the members of the ensemble. Very often more can be done in a shorter rehearsal with more concentrated effort.

Every conductor is responsible for giving his students suggestions about practicing. One of the most important of these is that two thirty-minute practice periods a day will usually be more beneficial than one period an hour in length. However, periods must not be so short that hard, concentrated work is impossible.

PROBLEMS AND PROCEDURES

1. Draw up a set of suggestions for maintaining discipline in a high school musical organization.

2. Draw up a plan for a rehearsal, indicating the time to be spent on each number and the type of rehearsal procedure to be used on each.

3. Which of the three methods of warming up do you prefer? Give your experiences in their use.

4. If you had a total weekly rehearsal time of five hours for one ensemble, how would you divide the time between full and sectional rehearsals?

5. Analyze the work of some of the most successful high school conductors you know. What are some of their practices in regard to the use of praise? Did they emphasize only the things done well or did they emphasize the things done poorly?

6. About how long would you advise a high school ensemble to rehearse at one time? Give reasons for your answer based upon your knowledge of the learning process.

SUGGESTIONS FOR FURTHER STUDY

CAIN, N. *Choral Music and Its Practice*, M. Witmark & Sons, 1932, Chap. IX.

COWARD, H. *Choral Technique and Interpretation*, Novello & Co., Ltd., London, pp. 8-18, 249-257.

DYKEMA and GEHRKENS. *The Teaching and Administration of High School Music*, C. C. Birchard & Company, 1941, Chap. XXVI.

HENDRICKS, W. E. "Send Them Away Singing", *Music Educators Journal*, Vol. XXIII, No. 6 (May, 1937).

HINDSLEY, M. *School Band and Orchestra Administration*, Boosey-Hawkes-Belwin, Inc., 1940, Chap. XII, XIII, XVI.

MURSELL and GLENN. *The Psychology of School Music Teaching*, Silver Burdett Company, 1938, Chap. III, IV.

PRESCOTT and CHIDESTER. *Getting Results with School Bands*, Paul A. Schmitt Music Company and Carl Fischer, Inc., 1938, Chap. VII, VIII.

WILSON, H. R. *Music in the High School*, Silver Burdett Company, 1941, Chap. VI, IX.

CHAPTER NINE

THE CONCERT

The natural outcome of weeks and months of rehearsals is the appearance of the ensemble before some public gathering. This may be considered to be of secondary importance to the educational benefits derived from the training but it is of decided importance and plans for it should receive as much of the conductor's attention as do his rehearsals. The music groups must understand that they are unlike most other activities in the school in that they often are expected to give freely of their time by singing and playing for the public which, in turn, is furnishing the opportunity for participation in music work. The music teacher often has to "sell" music to the public, something not required of other departments to the same degree.* This necessity means that results must be produced which will be heard and appreciated by the community, and also requires that the school music groups be exhibited to the public when community activities call for them.

All public appearances are important, even though the audience be extremely small. All engagements must be carefully thought out and fulfilled in the most efficient manner. The musical effects of the group are of extreme importance since it is from these that the greatest educational benefits are derived, but there are non-musical details which must be attended to if the most complete impression is to be made on the community.

The engagements which will have to be met vary in each community, but they are sure to include appearance in parades, at patriotic ceremonies, before civic clubs, societies and church groups, at athletic games, and they will involve complete ensembles, small groups and soloists. Each of these performing groups and individuals will present special problems in the proper selection of music, staging, transportation, and many other details. In addition to these performances, the music department of the school will present full length concerts of its own and the problems met in planning such concerts are so comprehensive that many of their solutions can be adapted for use in the minor engagements already listed. Such plans will vary to a certain extent in each situation, but there are enough problems common to all situations to make it worthwhile to consider them here. This discussion is not presented as a complete set of plans to be followed exclusively, but rather as a skeleton plan around which the conductor can "think through" a complete and efficient plan to fit any situation which may arise.

---

* For a further discussion of this problem see Chapter Twelve.

PRELIMINARY PLANS

Probably the majority of high school concerts are given jointly by all of the school music groups. As the music work progresses, it may be desirable for one group to give an entire concert. A plan for such a concert is much easier to formulate since it eliminates stage shifts and the necessity of dividing attention between several groups. A concert which features one organization supported by an organization of a different type provides variety, but retains more unity than school concerts which utilize all of the available school groups. Regardless of the type of concert being given, the following details must receive consideration.

1. *The appearance of the concert hall should be considered.* Whenever the public is invited into a school building, it becomes the responsibility of the whole school to put its best foot forward. When the music department is putting on a program the quality of the musical performance is predominantly important but the appearance of the whole school will be scrutinized and remarked upon. The auditorium in which the concert is to be given should be emptied of all non-essentials which would detract from its appearance. First of all, it should be meticulously clean. Simple decorations such as flowers or ivy and ferns will add greatly to the general appearance. This may serve as a project which will fit into the work of the art department or it may be done by members of the musical group under the supervision of a cooperative faculty member. A little ingenuity in the use of decorations can create a favorable atmosphere for any school performance.

Lighting facilities on the stage should be carefully checked. Groups which rehearse during the day rarely use lights and may neglect to experiment with them in order to find the most effective lighting. A stage which is too dark will detract from the general appearance of a group and will be particularly regrettable when uniforms or robes are used which require a particular kind of lighting in order to bring out the colors. When more than one ensemble is used, it may be necessary to switch the lighting for each group. Temporary spot-lights may need to be erected to eliminate shadows. Appearance is a major factor in a successful public performance of any kind and lighting is a major factor in appearance.

Pianos in the auditorium should be carefully tuned before a concert. When an instrumental soloist is used, he should tune to the piano before the concert so as to avoid the embarrassment of getting up before the audience and finding that the instrument cannot be tuned to the piano.

2. *A group of students and faculty members should be on hand to assist the conductor who should be free to give all of his attention to musical details.*

*Propriety — (1) the quality of being proper, fitting, or suitable; fitness. (2) conformity with what is proper or fitting. (3) conformity with accepted standards of manners or behavior.

THE CONCERT   115

Students may be used as ushers. Specific instructions should be given them as to how to do their job. Ushers should be responsible for closing doors before a number begins and not admitting anyone until the number is finished. The conductor would do well to mark a program for each usher, showing where a pause will be made to admit late comers. Playing while people are walking up and down the aisles can be eliminated in this way. Part of the conductor's job is to develop good audience habits in the entire school. A profound impression can be made on the public if students conduct themselves with propriety at concerts. Other faculty members should assist the conductor in this training.

When the concert is being given by more than one ensemble it means that the conductor will need assistance from faculty members in supervising the groups not on the stage. A faculty member should be assigned to each group, remaining with them until the time they go on the stage and meeting them as soon as they finish. Any groups assigned to a section of the auditorium after performing should be supervised by a faculty member.

3. *The matter of dress presents a major problem unless the ensemble is uniformed or robed.* The conductor can well give considerable thought to the problem of robes and uniforms. The robes of a choir should correspond to and set the mood for the music to be performed. The custom of using somber robes in the singing of light musical numbers seems ludicrous. In such cases it would seem better to have no robes at all. Some conductors are experimenting at choral concerts by presenting sacred music, sung by a robed choir, for the first part of the program and by presenting secular music, sung by a choir in uniform, evening, or street dress, for the second part of the program. For choral groups conductors should consider other types of uniforms besides robes.

Instrumental groups do not present the same problems as choral groups on account of the music which they play. For the orchestra, uniforms are not necessary. A similarity of dress, however, is advisable. For the band, some type of uniform seems essential. The thrill of a marching band in snappy uniforms is a memorable sight to young and old alike. The precedent of a colorfully uniformed marching band is carried over to the symphonic band. In truth, the brilliance of the instrumentation and the music to be played by a band seem to call for uniforms. The type of uniform for bands must be determined in each local situation. Since appearance is so tremendously important, every possible effort should be made to obtain some kind of uniformity.

Glee clubs present the easiest problem because satisfactory robes can be made by the members at a very low cost. In the spring, an all white ensemble can usually be provided by each individual member, but it is unwise to insist upon wearing a costume which will require new purchases. If this is done, the conductor may find some very valuable members missing at the concert only to discover later that they could not buy the necessary clothes and were ashamed to show up without them.

When uniformity cannot be obtained and the student may wear what he chooses, warning should be issued about avoiding loud colors, red ties and hair ribbons, white socks, unshined shoes and other such common articles of wearing apparel seen in every high school. Ensemble work requires subordination of the individual to the group in both performance and in appearance.

When uniforms are used there may still be difficulties because some student lacks a complete uniform or does not have his uniform pressed and clean. Such troubles can be largely eliminated by having an inspection the day of the concert and then leaving uniforms hung carefully in the school. This will eliminate the possibility of having them forgotten or ruined by rain the night of the concert.

(4.) *The final rehearsal* is the last contact the conductor has with his group before the concert and he should have ready a mimeographed list of directions which may be handed out to each member at the start of the rehearsal. The group can then go over this list and ask any necessary questions. Included in this list should be:

(a) Time and place to meet.

(b) What to do with instruments, cases, music and wraps at all times.

(c) Directions for warming up and tuning. If the orchestra is appearing, the help of a good string player should be obtained for tuning. If this is not possible, it is well to have the orchestra open the program so they can be tuned by the conductor before the concert starts. Strings which are tuned and then not played upon for an hour will be badly out of tune again.

(d) Entrances and exits should be reviewed. When several groups are participating this must be worked out very carefully beforehand so as to eliminate any unnecessarily long waits between groups.

(e) If the group is to be seated in the auditorium after performing, the exact location must be given and seats roped off.

(f) Instructions for acknowledging applause should be given. If the entire group is to rise they should be so instructed. Soloists in particular must be taught to bow, gracefully and calmly.

Stage managers must know just how many chairs and music racks are needed and must have made plans for setting up the stage for each group.

Librarians must have plans made for passing out and collecting music in the quickest possible way and should announce their plans to the group. Librarians should check all music the afternoon of the concert to be sure none is missing. Music should be placed in the order it will be played.

(5.) *The entire concert should be carefully timed* so that it is over within an hour and fifteen minutes to an hour and thirty minutes after it begins. This is usually quite long enough for an amateur program of even the highest quality. It is far better to have a concert too short than too long. When several groups are joining to give a concert much of the time may be wasted by entrances and exits. These waits are very tiring to the audience and must be counted into the total length of the program.

(6.) *The acoustics of a concert hall should be given special study* by the conductor. This study means that each group appearing in the concert must hold rehearsals in the auditorium so that the students will become accustomed to the conditions and so the conductor can make necessary adjustments. The conductor who never hears his groups from the vantage point of the audience is courting disaster. Some halls have brilliant acoustics and volume must be cut down. Other halls may magnify certain sections such as the percussion and then again a hall may reduce the sound of the back row. It is often possible to correct some of these defects by covering hard walls with curtains or by raising front curtains and increasing the height of the stage.

Choral organizations may increase their effectiveness in any auditorium by using raised platforms or risers, each row being at least six inches higher than the one in front of it.

In making preliminary plans for a concert, the conductor is warned again that the non-musical details of planning can add to or detract from the musical program and therefore, he should give them meticulous attention.

THE PROGRAM

When any school group appears in public it is exhibiting the results of its study and work during rehearsals. The primary aim of any school organization must of necessity be educational. The music which is used in rehearsals should be chosen with this in mind rather than with the aim of public entertainment. It is possible, however, by exercising great care, to realize both aims. Music can be found which is so worthwhile as to deserve inclusion in an educational program and still be extremely entertaining for the audience. A well-rounded program demands variety and so does a well-rounded education. There must be light moments in the rehearsal when music of an amusing character is used which will later add much zest to the program. A complete concert of this type of music is questionable, but a program of serious music usually needs some lighter numbers which emphasize entertainment values.

Suggestions relative to the building of complete band, orchestra, and choral programs will be found in the bibliography at the close of this chapter. The reader will also find helpful suggestions for program building and materials in the typical high school programs given in Appendix C. The concert in which several groups must be programmed presents additional problems, some of which are considered below.

1. When more than one group is appearing, the numbers to be performed by each group must have the same unity and variety as does an entire program. Each unit must be complete in itself.

2. When more than one group is appearing, consideration should be given to the order of appearance. This order should be decided by the ability of each group and its appeal to the audience. Having a weak group appear after a strong group is not recommended for obvious reasons. A good opening and a brilliant ending are essentials. Programming a vocal group between two instrumental groups provides variety and gives an opportunity for rest to the instrumentalists.

3. In arranging any school program, consideration must be given to the endurance of the participants. The complete contemplated program should be gone through at one rehearsal to test the reaction of the group. The conductor will not want to approach a difficult number near the end of a long program only to discover that his group has become overtired and is likely to break down. This can easily happen with immature vocalists and brass players. It will usually be found that the audience tires along with the players and so it is advisable to include the heaviest numbers in the first half of the program and the lighter numbers in the final portion. This also implies that the final numbers should be less lengthy than the initial numbers.

4. Numbers which tax the ensemble to the utmost in rehearsals are usually dangerous to use in public appearances. If they are used, a few easier numbers should precede them to allow time for nervousness to disappear. The use of an easy opening number is highly recommended in any performance.

5. Careful thought should be given to the selection of a brilliant closing number. Such a closing erases, to a certain extent at least, memories of any previous mishaps. When several groups are appearing, a joint closing number provides a most thrilling climax.

6. When two groups are giving the concert, it is wise to program an intermission between the two, allowing time for shifts. When three or

more groups are participating, the time needed for making shifts will provide intermissions but these had best not be programmed since they are too numerous.

7. If a program is carefully planned as a complete unit, the use of encores will disrupt the unity and may best be placed at the end of the regular program. An excessive number of encores delivered on the slightest pretext detracts from, rather than adds to, the total effect of the program.

8. The placing of high school soloists in the program must receive thoughtful consideration. A brass or vocal soloist in particular should not be scheduled after a taxing ensemble number nor before a difficult number in which the ensemble needs his support. The question of endurance also makes it advisable to schedule all soloists at a time before fatigue has begun to set in. The soloist often appreciates being allowed to refrain from much participation in the ensemble number directly preceding his appearance.

To thoroughly test his endurance, the program as planned should be played through in a rehearsal and the soloist permitted to appear before the ensemble. This will also help to develop confidence, especially if the ensemble members are kind enough to lend encouragement.

9. Variety, unity, and effective arrangement are prime essentials for the format of any musical program.

There are many types of programs which can be used, from the single sheet mimeographed program to the expensive covered program with cuts of the musical groups appearing, including program notes. Financial restrictions will probably play a part in the final selection, but an ingenious conductor can make any program look effective if he can get the cooperation of a good printer. If at all possible, the personnel of each participating group should be included, as the students like to see their names on the program. Likewise, parents are pleased when they see the names of their children on printed programs.

Information which should appear on all programs, in addition to the musical numbers include: the school and organizations giving the concert, the city, the state, and the building in which the concert is being given, the date and time of the performance, also the name of the conductor or conductors.

PROBLEMS AND PROCEDURES

1. Attend a high school concert or try to recall one which you have attended, and make a report on the strengths and weaknesses in planning which were apparent to you. What suggestions would you make to improve the program and the smoothness with which it was performed?

2. Draw up plans for decorating any high school auditorium with which you are familiar. Give the approximate cost of your decorations.

3. Draw up a list of instructions for ushers.

4. Design a simple choral robe and figure its cost, giving exact figures. Discuss the appropriateness of different types of band uniforms.

5. Draw up a list of final concert instructions to be given to members of a high school organization with which you are acquainted. Distinguish between the directions made for that particular group and those which would apply to any group giving a concert.

6. Collect a variety of high school concert programs and study them. Then make suggestions for improvement. Estimate the cost of materials and cost of printing per thousand of several different types. If possible, consult a printer regarding layouts and costs.

SUGGESTIONS FOR FURTHER STUDY

CAIN, N. *Choral Music and Its Practice,* M. Witmark & Sons, 1932, Chap. XIII.

GEHRKENS, K. W. *Essentials in Conducting,* Oliver Ditson Company, Inc., 1919, Chap. XIV.

GOLDMAN, E. F. *Band Betterment,* Carl Fischer, Inc., 1934, Chap. XII.

GREENE, H. P. *Interpretation in Song,* The Macmillan Company, Ltd., London, 1931, Part V.

PRESCOTT and CHIDESTER. *Getting Results with School Bands,* Paul A. Schmitt Music Company and Carl Fischer, Inc., 1938, Chapter XIX.

WARD, A. *Music Education for High Schools,* American Book Company, 1941, Chap. XIV.

WILSON, H. R. *Music in the High School,* Silver Burdett Company, 1941, Chap. IV and V.

CHAPTER TEN

COMPETITION-FESTIVALS

There is much to be said for and against participation in our present competition-festivals but the conductor would do well to take a realistic position and admit that in spite of his own beliefs, he may find it necessary to participate in such an event and therefore he should understand the problems involved. The teacher who has had some experience with competition-festivals, who understands their problems, and who has seen at first hand the good and bad effects which participation has on a school organization, will be in a position to judge the value of such participation on the basis of factual evidence.

The conductor who has considered all facts and who has decided that competition-festivals are a worthwhile activity, should ask himself the following questions relative to the participation of his own group in such an affair.

1. *What are the standards of the class in which my groups will participate?*

Standards are determined by the groups participating and will, therefore, vary considerably. Certain sections of a state have higher standards than others, some states have higher standards than their neighbors, and this variation is just as great in National Regional Competition-festivals. When comparisons are made, when the contest element enters, the wise competitor will want to know something about the quality of his competition.

2. *Approximately how will my groups rate in such a competition-festival?*

The realistic conductor who can answer the first question satisfactorily will be able to give a fairly good answer to the second one, possibly erring on the side of predicting too low a rating rather than one too high.

Why is it important that an estimate of rating be made? Because competition-festivals provide a basis for comparison of the work of different schools. If the rating is too low, the effect may be to discourage rather than encourage the group. One of the strongest arguments for the competition-festival is that it will raise the standard of work since it will recognize superior work and point out inferior work. If this aim is to be realized, judges must give realistic ratings and not rate obviously inferior work as good or excellent. It is unfair to ask a judge to encourage participating groups and then to include groups whose work is so far below standard that in all honesty the judge must give a discouragingly low rating. If ratings are to carry the significance attached to them in other fields of measurement, they should be accurate.

If the conductor of a group in its second year of existence finds that his group would be in a section with ten of the best in the state, would he be wise to ask to have his group compared with such mature performers, and what effect would it have on his group? If the conductor talks it over with the group ahead of time, explaining that the rating will probably be low because of conditions not under their control, and allows the group to decide whether, under the circumstances, they should enter, then the effects may not be bad. The groups who enter competitions without knowing the strength of the competitors and who expect to get a much higher rating than would be possible even with the most lenient judge, will suffer drastically. The conductor is the one to be blamed for such an unfortunate experience. He has not evaluated the standards of the competitors, and has not made a true estimate of the rating which his own group can hope to attain.

In most competition-festivals it is possible for a group to participate and receive the constructive criticisms of the judges without being rated. Such a group is said to be playing for criticism only. This procedure should be considered by immature groups since it makes possible participation in a very stimulating and helpful activity without exposing the group to the disheartening consequences of an extremely low rating.

PROBLEMS IN TAKING GROUPS TO COMPETITION-FESTIVALS

Participation in a competition-festival creates many problems in administration and organization. These will vary with each situation but consideration of most of the following problems usually is involved.

1. Transportation

The three possibilities here are to go by train, by bus, or by private automobile.

(a) When going by train, arrangements must be made for transporting the personnel and equipment from the station to the festival headquarters or to the quarters in which the group is to be housed.

(b) When going by bus, arrangements should be made to provide for the use of the bus at all times after arriving at the destination so that no problems of transportation from housing headquarters to festival headquarters will be involved.

(c) When going by private automobile, insurance laws must be investigated. As a general rule, when a private car is let out for hire, the liability insurance is invalidated. If the use of the car is donated this is not true. It is necessary to give the drivers of private cars a list of directions so that there will be no question as to the procedure on arrival at festival headquarters. Drivers usually act as chaperons. When they do serve in this capacity their duties may be made clear on the list of directions.

② Finances

A tentative budget should be set up showing costs of housing, meals, transportation, entry fees, and other incidentals. Then there can be a concerted drive to raise the amount of money needed.

The ideal solution to the financial problem is to have the Board of Education pay all expenses. This is rarely done but the Board will often provide funds for certain specific parts of the budget such as entry fees, chaperons' expenses, or transportation of equipment.

Concerts by the musical organizations, benefit movies, tag days, contributions from civic organizations, bridge parties, and various other methods have been used to raise money for competition-festival expenses.

The participants are often asked to begin a savings fund at the beginning of the school year so that they may pay for some specific part of the budget such as entry fees, meals, or housing expenses. If, at the beginning of the school year, each member of the organization turns in ten cents a week to the treasurer this will be sufficient to pay for his own housing and some of his meals when festival time arrives. This can be refunded if the trip is not made.

Many schools have formed clubs such as the Band Mothers' Club, which assume the responsibility of raising money for trips, instruments, and uniforms. The conductor assumes an active role in directing the policies of such organizations.

③ Housing

In many instances, trips will be of such length that an over-night stay is necessary. Participants are housed in hotels or private homes and reservations must be made as early as possible if satisfactory accommodations are to be obtained. Since several students will occupy the same room, room-mates should be decided upon and the list forwarded to the hotel at which reservations have been made. Then when the group arrives, rooms will have been assigned and a great deal of confusion will have been eliminated.

Hotel accommodations are by far the most satisfactory since the entire group may be housed together and can be properly supervised. If private homes are used, it is absolutely necessary to have the address and telephone number of each student. It is also necessary to set various times during the day when all persons will assemble for a brief meeting at which time altered plans may be explained.

When traveling to the festival by bus or private automobile it is often possible to spend the night in a town near the festival city. This arrangement may be more satisfactory because there will be no other school groups to complicate administrative matters.

4. Chaperons

Chaperons who understand clearly just what is expected of them are an absolute essential. Parents or faculty members can serve in this capacity but it is often wise to have parents chaperon other children than their own since they have a tendency to allow their own children special privileges. Rules which are made for the entire organization may not be suspended by parental decree. As a rule no chaperon should have charge of more than five students.

Chaperons should be informed in order that they can answer questions of the students concerning the program of activities and help them in every way possible. They should not assume a dictatorial attitude but at the same time they must be alert to check those students who have not learned to discipline themselves on such occasions.

5. Equipment

Equipment includes instruments, music racks, music, and uniforms.

Many competition-festivals will agree to furnish certain heavy instruments such as tubas, string basses, and percussion instruments. This arrangement makes for convenience but the conductor should realize that students cannot perform as well on strange instruments as they can on their own.

There will be many occasions on which promised equipment is not available for a variety of reasons. The safest procedure, although not the most convenient, is to carry all needed equipment. For vocal groups equipment will include collapsible risers.

A folding music rack can be carried by each player. This will insure having an adequate supply on the festival stage as well as for any rehearsals.

Music can be cared for by the librarians and passed out or placed on the racks just before it is needed. This is usually more satisfactory than having each individual responsible for transporting his own music.

Each participant should be made responsible for his uniform or choir robe. If apparel is packed for shipment, it should be hung out immediately upon arrival at the festival, so that all wrinkles will be removed. Many groups prefer to hang all uniforms and robes on a specially built rack which can be fitted into a bus or private car.

6. Rules

Conduct at a competition-festival is often indicative of the kind of self-discipline being developed by the school. Students should understand that at such an event they are representing their school and that their actions must be governed accordingly. Rules there must be, but the fewer the better. Rules which are made should be enforced. Trips in following years will be made much easier if this is done on the very first trip. Students who do not have the self-discipline to conduct themselves properly cannot be expected to be taken along on trips where such self-discipline is essential.

7. Legal responsibility

Since the music organization in a competition-festival is representing a school, the legal responsibility of the Board of Education must be given careful consideration. This may be found to include responsibility for any accidents enroute or at the festival. When the Board is not willing to assume such a tremendous responsibility it is sometimes possible to have each parent sign a release statement. Some schools will take out a blanket insurance policy covering the entire group for the trip. The importance of going over this whole matter with a legal representative of the Board of Education cannot be overemphasized. The conductor should be sure that he is not legally liable for any mishaps which may occur.

8. Final directions

A mimeographed list of directions given to each student will help eliminate much of the confusion so often seen at competition-festivals. This set of directions will give the entire schedule for the day, specifying where each event is to be held, at what time participants are to meet, and the place they will meet. Directions should be given in the order they are to be executed:

1. Report to the ——— hotel and go to your assigned room.
2. Hang up your uniform. If it is quite wrinkled, have it pressed.
3. Wash up and be in the lobby of the hotel at ——— o'clock. Be in uniform and have your instrument and music rack.

etc.

Somewhere in these directions it is well to include a reminder about hearing other groups and soloists perform. This is one of the greatest opportunities of the competition-festival and one of the best reasons for its continuance. Students are more likely to listen to other groups if they are told to hear certain specific organizations which are known to be among the better ones in their class.

9. Miscellaneous

The conductor should be thoroughly familiar with the rules governing the competition-festival in which his group is appearing. This will include classification rules, which often vary; eligibility of the entire ensemble and of individual members such as post-graduates; rules governing required and selective music to be performed by each class; entrance deadline date; the number of minutes allowed for each performance; whether there will be a sight-reading contest; and any others which have been sent to him. There have been many instances when groups have spent a lot of time and money getting to a competition-festival only to be disqualified for some obvious infraction of the rules with which the conductor should have been familiar.

It is important that all participating groups be on time. If the local committee draws up a schedule, soloists and ensembles should follow it. Failure to do so may result in a reduced time allowance or disqualification.

Whenever possible, attendance at a competition-festival should be so planned that it will not interfere with the regular school program. There is small justification for taking students out of other classes to hold extra rehearsals.

Judges are expected to offer helpful suggestions. In order to do this they should be furnished with a conductor's score for each number to be performed. Failure to do this, or the substitution of some incomplete type of score will result in fewer valuable criticisms.

The participating group should not be led to believe that they will receive the highest rating, even when the conductor feels that such a rating will be awarded. The effect of getting a higher rating than was expected is encouraging but the reverse sometimes has bad effects. The conductor who continually questions the decisions of the judges had better examine his own musical judgment.

PREPARATION FOR THE COMPETITION-FESTIVAL

The following problems are those which the conductor must face in his capacity as musical head of an ensemble entering a competition-festival. Many of the problems already discussed may be delegated to others; in fact, should be largely so delegated in order that the conductor may be free to devote his time to the thing he alone is capable of doing.

1. *The selection of proper music is of major importance.*

Most competition-festivals designate one number which all groups are to perform although some will name several from which each conductor may make a choice.

In addition to the required number, each group is permitted to perform certain numbers of its own choosing, selected from a large list of approved music. In making selections the conductor often wonders whether he should choose easy or difficult music. Experience has shown that it is wise to use a grade of music which can be performed well. A good performance of difficult music may be rated higher than a good performance of easy music; however, a poor performance of difficult music will not receive the same credit as a well executed presentation of easier music. A finished performance of the simplest music is more convincing than a hit and miss attempt at something obviously too difficult.

Every group in a competition-festival desires to make the best impression possible. In order to do this weak sections must be covered up and strong sections given prominence. Music should be selected which will make this possible. If the tenor section is weak, select music with an easy tenor part. If the violin section is strong, feature it. If there is an excellent soloist, find a number in which he can be used. Avoid those selections which feature soloists who have not had experience under the strain of competition. The experienced conductor spends much time trying over numbers until those which have the best effect are found.

Numbers chosen should fit into a well-rounded program. An easy opening number, which the group knows perfectly, will result in added confidence for the remainder of the program. An effective closing number is just as essential in a short program as it is in a long one. If the required number is an overture, the choice number should be in another form if possible.

The conductor of an instrumental group will be able to obtain a more finished performance if he selects a number which has a full score. If, for some reason, a number which does not have a full score must be used, the conductor should consider making a full score for himself. The added results will justify the time spent.

2. *The conductor should study the adjudicator's sheet to be used in the competition-festival.*

If rehearsals are conducted so as to realize the aims suggested in Chapter Five groups will rate high as measured by any adjudicator's sheet since all musical performances are judged on how well those aims are realized. Experience has shown that school music groups are most often rated down on two essential elements: tone quality and intonation.

It should be understood that essentials of musical performance are not being stressed just to obtain a high rating in a competition-festival but because they are necessary to the success of any musical endeavor, both from the standpoint of performance and appreciation.

3. *The music to be used should be presented in public several times before the appearance at the competition-festival.*

Each public appearance will uncover weak spots which were not evident in rehearsals. Public appearances result in added confidence on the part of the performers.

The reaction of the audience on such occasions should be carefully noted and the criticisms of competent musicians sought. The finest conductor in the world cannot hear and see everything that is taking place. He will be able to spot the more obvious errors, but since he is seeking perfection he should use every available means of discovering and eliminating all defects. The use of a recording machine is another means of discovering errors.

(4.) *Pay attention to sight-reading.*

Most state and national regional competition-festivals include a test in sight-reading. The conductor should be familiar with the routine followed and should have his students read a great deal of music using the procedures which they will be required to follow.

The conductor is allowed about two minutes to look over the music, usually two numbers. In the case of instrumental groups, a march and an overture are usually used. Choral groups may be given one accompanied and one unaccompanied number. After this the participants are given from two to three minutes to look over the music, during which time the conductor may call attention to tricky repeats, cut-offs, holds, tempi, and other important points, also to assign solo parts to the best readers. He is permitted to whistle or sing parts so as to indicate tempo or the solution of a rhythmic problem but he may not play an instrument in order to make such illustrations. The choral conductor is usually prohibited from singing but may clap rhythms. Whenever possible, the conductor should learn the exact procedures to be used and practice them with his group. It is obvious that only a fine accompanist will be of any help in the choral reading test.

(5.) *Appearance is an important factor in any public performance.*

Correct posture, so necessary for good playing or singing, is the first requisite for making a fine appearance. If this has been made habitual, there will be no relapses because of forgetfulness.

Uniform dress is best obtained by using robes or uniforms but if this is not possible, be sure that lack of uniformity is compensated for by neatness. The conductor is very often an offender in the matter of dress. The conductor of a uniformed group is obligated to appear in an appropriate uniform. Band members should not wear hats in an indoor performance.

A good seating arrangement will give the effect of balance and symmetry. It is disconcerting to see one half of the stage with many more persons on it than the other half. Choir members should be arranged by height as far as possible. Band conductors can seat their members in semicircles. There should be a uniform distance between players and desks.

Instruments should be well polished. Some bands adopt a certain finish, such as gold lacquer, and buy all instruments in this finish.

The uniformed group has a definite color scheme. Accessories should, whenever possible, blend into this scheme. A good effect can be obtained by covering the folios with paper which matches the uniform and then using open back music racks so that the color scheme can be seen. Gaudy colors are as aggravating to the eye as are a variety of sharply contrasting colors. The musical performance is an aesthetic experience which is enjoyed through the auditory senses but it is well to give the visual senses some consideration.

6. *Sectional rehearsals are, at times, more valuable than full rehearsals.*

The conductor who must choose between daily full rehearsals and no sectionals or fewer full rehearsals and some sectionals would do well to consider the latter choice. Clarity of parts, balance, and intonation within a section are best obtained in a sectional rehearsal. This is particularly true for the conductor who finds it difficult to hear everything that goes on in a full rehearsal. The inner parts make or break a performance. These parts can best be worked out in rehearsals of small groups. It is highly desirable to hold such rehearsals soon after a number has been introduced so that a correct performance can be obtained before bad habits are established.

In connection with extra rehearsals, it is well to bear in mind that the competition-festival presents an opportunity to exhibit the type of work done during the entire school year. Some of the objections to participating in such an event are brought about by conductors who schedule many extra rehearsals during the month preceding the festival, often taking students out of regular classes and disrupting the normal school schedule in other ways, in an effort to make up for work which should have been done earlier in the year or in order to produce results which the time allotment and equipment of the school do not justify. A school which schedules one rehearsal a week and has no music in the elementary grades should not expect to receive as high a rating as the school which recognizes the importance of music and makes necessary arrangements for the development of a strong program. The groups which will receive the highest ratings are not those which will have held the greatest number of rehearsals during the month before the competition-festival.

7. *Compositions may need to be rearranged to fit the group performing them.*

This requires a good knowledge of arranging and is too big a question to discuss here. Nevertheless, it should be made clear to the conductor that this is a practice indulged in by many of the best school music groups in the country, particularly in the band field where so many orchestral numbers have been arranged for band. In a number of this type, it is permissible and desirable to shift parts from weak sections to strong sections as long as no distortion results. In choral groups, a few altos are often assigned to bolster the high tenor tones and then return to their own part. In orchestra, a solo assigned to the oboe may be more effective if played by another instrument when the oboist is a poor player.

Simplifying parts is necessary for ensembles in which immature and mature players are grouped together. The general practice is to assign some strong players to each part and then have the weaker players play only the parts they can handle. These players will stop playing during soft sustained passages which require fine intonation. A very sound educational principle is being observed here. Each player is doing work at his present level of development. This leads to much finer ensemble playing.

A SIMPLIFIED SECOND VIOLIN PART

8. *Careful thought should be given to the problems which will be encountered at the competition-festival.* These will vary slightly but those listed below will be common to all such events.

a. The acoustics of the hall in which the group will perform should be given careful consideration. It is, of course, impossible to change the acoustical characteristics of a hall but the performance of the group can be altered so as to get the best results from an acoustical standpoint.

In order to determine the acoustical properties, an effort should be made to hear other groups performing in the hall. The stage itself should be carefully examined. Some stages have heavy curtains which absorb much of the sound or have high ceilings so that some of the sound goes up rather than out. In this case, the group should be placed as far forward on the stage as possible. The group is usually seated behind a curtain but as soon as the curtain is drawn, the participants can move to the very front of the stage. On some stages, the rear row of the band or orchestra finds itself next to a concrete wall or wood partition separating the stage from the gymnasium. Such a background tends to magnify the sound of the instruments nearest to it, particularly if these are trumpets or percussion instruments. In instances like this it may be necessary to advise these players never to play above a mezzo-forte and to watch the conductor for other changes which may be necessary after the performance begins.

Music in some halls sounds extremely brilliant. This condition can be used to good advantage by eliminating the top of the dynamic range. Better blend and balance usually result. This type of hall may magnify the sounds of certain instruments. If the conductor is able to hear several other groups performing in the hall he can discover such distortions and advise his group accordingly.

The immature group may be greatly upset when the sounds they hear coming from their instruments are different than the ones they are used to hearing at home. Very often they find it difficult to hear themselves and other sections and get the impression that they are playing too lightly. This will often happen in a large hall and the conductor may get the same impression and consequently ask for more volume. This is a bad mistake because it invariably results in forcing, lack of balance, and poor blending. It is safe to cut down the dynamic range but it is not safe to try to extend it. Participants should be cautioned not to play or sing louder in a new hall than they do at home regardless of the sounds they hear. The truth is that the sound is projected out from the stage and the effect as heard by the audience will be good.

(b) The group should meet together at least forty-five minutes before they are scheduled to perform in order to tune, warm-up, and review important details.

Each organization should have developed a tuning routine which produces the best results for them and takes the least time. It is advised that no new, untried procedure be used at such a time in an effort to produce better results.

Likewise, a warming-up routine should have been developed which has been found to produce good results.

Last minute details such as distribution of music, review of manner of getting on and off the stage, what to do after the performance is over with regard to instruments and uniforms, can be tended to at this time.

Another important duty of the conductor at this meeting is to get his group in the right frame of mind. This means that the participants must be concentrating on the job to be done. It is a mistake, however, to encourage nervousness and tension by too serious a manner. The conductor should not reflect such tension and if anything, should attempt to create an atmosphere of ease and confidence. He should pay particular attention to those who have solo parts. A smile, a pat on the back and at times, a good joke, will produce a healthier atmosphere than a frown, a grumpy voice, and threats.

A cheerful and confident attitude on the part of the conductor is especially important in the sight-reading test. This test is quite a strain on the participants and they will want to do their best. The authors have seen conductors stop their group and call them down for making a mistake. Such practice only adds tension and when the passage is tried again the result is usually worse. The experienced conductor will impress on his group the fact that the numbers to be played are no more difficult than those they have been sight-reading during the year at home.

Procedures After the Competition-Festival

A group entering a competition-festival will want to know whether the time and money spent were justified. There is a great deal of stimulation before the event but what are the after-effects? The conductor should watch carefully for these and guide discussions along some of the following helpful lines:

1. What did we see or hear that we can use to advantage? In this discussion, do the participants show evidences of increased discrimination as the result of having heard other groups and soloists? Have them make a list of suggestions and consider adopting those which have value. These suggestions will be a concrete example of value received. The learning which takes place within each individual through having heard groups from other schools is often more important than the criticisms of the judges.

2. What weaknesses did we discover to exist in our own organization as evidenced by the judges' criticisms and by our own comparisons with groups from other schools? What can we do to strengthen these weaknesses? This will often result in an improved instrumentation, uniforms, and an improved plan of organization which will enable the group to make a better showing in the future.

3. What other values did we receive from participating, exclusive of musical values? Did we meet any interesting people from other schools? Did we see anything of historical importance at the host city or in our travels to and from the competition-festival?

4. Were our experiences important enough to share with our schoolmates? Could we make up some reports which would be of interest to other classes or civic organizations of the town?

5. Finally, taking all these things into consideration, the work involved and the expense, do we wish to participate again next year?

The conductor who proceeds along these lines will be able to answer those critics who say that the only reason for attendance at a competition-festival is to win a prize. Participation should be justifiable from an educational point of view. The conductor must collect concrete evidence to show that competition-festivals foster worthwhile educational results.

Problems and Procedures

1. Draw up a list of final directions to be handed to chaperons, outlining clearly their duties at the competition-festival. Draw up a similar list for the students or combine the two, if possible.

2. Draw up a tentative budget for taking a group of seventy-five instrumentalists to the city in which your state competition-festival is held. Use the town in which you are now located as the starting point. Compare your figures with those drawn up by others in the class.

3. Draw up a list of rules which are to be observed on a trip to a competition-festival.

4. What are the rules governing your state competition-festival?

5. Select two good contest numbers for any group with which you are familiar. What parts, if any, must be simplified?

6. Select some moderately easy number, study it for three minutes and then make a list of things you would call to the attention of your group in a sight-reading competition.

Suggestions for Further Study

CHRISTY, VAN A. *Glee Club and Chorus,* G. Schirmer, Inc., 1940, Chap. VII.

GEHRKENS and DYKEMA. *The Teaching and Administration of High School Music,* C. C. Birchard & Company, 1941, Chap. XXII.

PRESCOTT and CHIDESTER. *Getting Results with School Bands,* Paul A. Schmitt Music Company and Carl Fischer, Inc., 1938, Chap. XX.

The bulletin, *State and National School Music Competition-Festivals,* published by the Music Educators National Conference at 64 E. Jackson Blvd., Chicago, Illinois, should be examined thoroughly. The music lists are invaluable for all schools, regardless of participation in competition-festivals.

WILSON, H. R. *Music in the High School,* Silver Burdett Company, 1941, Chap. V.

CHAPTER ELEVEN

OTHER DUTIES OF THE CONDUCTOR

The major portion of the high school conductor's job has now been briefly covered. There will be, however, a large number of other duties stemming out directly from the main job of conducting choral and instrumental groups. These duties may at times assume major importance and may consume even more time than do the main rehearsals. The mere fact that a person can wield a baton will, at times, invite duties of which many conductors would be glad to be relieved. Only the most important of these miscellaneous duties will be considered here, and then very briefly, since a full discussion of them would require more space than can be devoted to them in this book. The conductor who finds himself faced with any of these duties would do well to consult the bibliography at the end of this chapter.

ASSEMBLY PROGRAMS

The importance assigned to the assembly period varies according to the school administrator. To many it is the most vital period of the school week while others think so little of its value as to eliminate it entirely or to hold only a few during an entire school year.

Should the conductor obtain a position in a school where the assembly is of major importance he should immediately confer with the administrator and try to gain an understanding of aims and functions of the assembly. It is extremely important, for example, to know whether the assembly period is conceived to be primarily a recreational period with the emphasis on entertainment, whether it is educational in the sense that the emphasis is on giving instruction, or whether it is a combination of both. When there is no clear-cut philosophy formulated by the school administrator, the conductor must of necessity formulate his own. It is certainly safe to say that when assembly periods are scheduled, regardless of their aim, the conductor will be called upon to perform certain duties.

The most important of these duties will be to lead assembly singing. This may call for one or two songs or it may call for an entire period devoted to singing. It is obvious that in this type of work, problems are met which differ from those met in the ensemble rehearsals. Anyone who has seen a good community song leader at work will immediately be struck by the difference between his attitude and that of the usual choir conductor. His sole aim seems to be to create enthusiasm, to encourage a breaking down of reserve, to get everyone so happy and spirited that even

134

the off-key singer forgets his self-consciousness and joins in the fun. Such must necessarily be one of his aims since he is working with a group, many of whom very rarely sing and often have small or no interest in music itself. Nevertheless, the enthusiastic song leader who is an excellent conductor may achieve fine musical results in assembly singing. The more formal manner of the rehearsal room would be utterly futile in creating an atmosphere conducive to a successful assembly sing. It is quite possible for a person to be a fine conductor of assembly sings and a weak conductor of specialized music groups, and even more possible, that the successful specialized group conductor may be a mediocre or poor assembly song leader. Assembly singing can often serve as a stimulus for interesting the student body to become members of music organizations in the school.

The accompaniment for assembly singing is of great importance for a strong accompaniment is usually needed in order to promote full participation. Students will often join in when they find that the accompaniment is strong enough to make their voices less conspicuous. It is then possible to tone down the accompaniment once the ice has been broken. The school orchestra will usually be the most satisfying accompaniment medium, but lacking this, some of the brass players may be used along with a competent pianist. Needless to say, rehearsals with the accompanying body must be held before the assembly sing in order to set tempi, determine the amount of introduction to be played for each number, the verses to be sung, and other such details.

When any extensive singing is done in the assembly, material must be provided. In many situations the most satisfactory means is the purchase of an adequate number of a better-type community song book. The book should contain melodious songs that students enjoy singing today; it should contain songs which give opportunity for the development of part-singing; it should contain rounds, seasonal songs, and action songs. It is often well to buy a book that can be used in the general music classes and general chorus as well as the assembly. If possible, a school should have more than one book for assembly singing in order that there may be a wide variety of interesting material. There should be enough copies for each student to have a book, if possible. There should be at least one book for every two students. Assembly books should be durable and attractive for they are an important part of assembly singing.

To avoid the distribution of books some conductors have used song slides for assembly singing. Since most schools own a slide projector it is also argued that slides are less expensive than books. However, slides have definite limitations. The darkened room produces discipline problems. Interpretative effects through conducting become most difficult to obtain. Part-singing is not feasible. Moreover, the material available on song slides is somewhat meager and the assembly that sings only from slides will have a deficient musical diet. They may be used to advantage for some special feature or program, but to use slides exclusively is questionable practice.

If material is mimeographed for assembly singing to save expenses care must be taken by the conductor that he is not infringing upon the copyright law. It is absolutely unethical to mimeograph materials, either words or music, which is covered by copyright unless permission is received from the publisher.[1] It is perfectly permissible to mimeograph words and music which are in public domain but this material is extremely limited. Mimeographed material may supplement the use of books but it can by no means replace them if a satisfactory program of assembly singing is to be carried on.

All groups, musical and non-musical, seem to like to follow a conductor. The assembly sing should be conducted, using enlarged motions, so definitely made that the group is held together perfectly. Efforts should be made by the leader to obtain variation in tempo and dynamics in order that some interpretative effects may be secured by the entire assembly.

THE OPERETTA

The operetta is still one of the most popular types of musical entertainment, and in many schools it is a yearly event which is the most important school activity of the year. Much can be said both for and against putting on an operetta, but when the tradition has been established over a period of years, the new teacher must follow along or replace it with other activities which will be accepted by the student body. It is quite well agreed that the operetta is a splendid tonic for putting life into a music department which has been dormant. It creates tremendous enthusiasm among the students and parents, and does not require as long a period of preparation for its production as do the specialized vocal and instrumental groups for their performances.

The conducting problems created are not new, only slightly different. It is necessary to synchronize the chorus, soloists, and accompaniment, and when the latter is furnished by the inexperienced school orchestra the conductor will have his hands full. The conductor who plans to present an operetta should study with great care the books on the subject listed at the close of this chapter.

---

[1] *A Business Handbook*, Music Exhibitors Association, Music Educators National Conference, Chicago. This handbook may be secured from the M.E.N.C. free of charge with the compliments of the Association. It explains the copyright law, gives valuable suggestions for ordering music, and contains an annotated list of publishers.

THE MARCHING BAND

The band conductor will, in almost all instances, be responsible for developing a marching band. There are rare instances when another instructor in the school who has a knowledge of military routine will take over the drilling of the band, making the conductor responsible only for selecting and working out music to fit each special occasion. There is little connection between conducting and marching drill. Because of this, the conductor who is in charge of this work must have special training, either obtained by experience in a marching band, or by studying what has been said by marching band authorities.

STUDENT CONDUCTORS

High school students enjoy conducting and can be taught to do quite a satisfactory job, at least in respect to the development of baton technic. The conductor should offer help to those whose talent and interest warrant it. When enough skill has been developed, opportunities for public appearances should be provided. Appearances by ensembles before the school assemblies can be handled efficiently by a student conductor. Every public concert might well feature at least one or two of the easier numbers conducted by a student.

One of the most valuable contributions which the student conductor can make comes before the important public concert. The conductor himself, at several rehearsals before the concert, should listen to his groups from a seat in the auditorium. This cannot be recommended too strongly as it is only in this way that a clear concept of how the groups sound to the audience can be formed. A student conductor can be put in charge of the group while the conductor is doing the listening. The conductor will soon realize that he has been amply repaid for the time spent in training student conductors by just this service alone.

PRE-HIGH SCHOOL MUSIC

Music study in the elementary and intermediate schools may not be a direct responsibility of the high school conductor but it bears such an important relationship to his work that some mention of it should be made. The conducting problems of the music teacher in these schools are very similar to those of the high school teacher, and the preceding discussions should be helpful to them, also.

The ultimate success of the high school music program depends not only upon the ability of the conductor but also upon the background in music established by the students before entering high school. This is true of all phases of both vocal and instrumental music. It is the pre-high school training which develops understanding, skills, and interest. The high school conductor should therefore interest himself not only in seeing that there is adequate musical instruction in the earlier years, but also that it is the type of instruction which will lead to desirable outcomes. A program of music study which leads to the formation of bad habits and negative interest will make more difficult the job of the high school conductor.

A strong course of grade school vocal music is the first step in developing a background conducive to a more successful high school music program. Such a plan is of immeasurable value for both the instrumental and vocal programs. The instrumentalists who have gained a knowledge of the musical score and have learned to express their musical feelings in singing will have laid a fine foundation for good instrumental performance.

When there is any pre-high school music course, the high school conductor should be acquainted with the teaching approaches used and the kind and amount of work covered. It is only in this way that he can build intelligently on what has already been done and it is only through such correlated effort that the most satisfactory results can be realized in high school music.

PROBLEMS AND PROCEDURES

1. Plan several musical programs for the assembly built around some central idea.

2. Make a list of songs to be used in an assembly sing. Indicate those which are to be used primarily for their educational value and those which are used primarily for their entertainment value. Defend your choice of songs from the standpoint of variety, securing interest, text, range, and general difficulty.

3. What uses would you make of a public address system and a movie projector in the assembly program?

4. What departments in the school should cooperate in presenting an operetta? In what way?

5. What are the educational values of a marching band? Are these values more closely related to the music department or the physical education department? Is the marching band largely justified by the training it affords its members or by its "spectator appeal"?

6. If you were in charge of a high school instrumental program and found that there had been no pre-high school music, would you attempt to establish vocal or instrumental work first? Why?

SUGGESTIONS FOR FURTHER STUDY

ASSEMBLY PROGRAMS

BEATTIE, McCONATHY and MORGAN. *Music in the Junior High School*, Silver Burdett Company, 1930, Chap. XIV.

GEHRKENS, K. W. *Music in the Junior High School*, C. C. Birchard & Company, 1936, Chap. V.

WILSON, H. R. *Music in the High School*, Silver Burdett Company, 1941, Chap. IV.

OPERETTA PRODUCTION

BEACH, F. *Preparation and Presentation of the Operetta*, Oliver Ditson Company, Inc., 1930.

JONES and WILSON. *Musico-Dramatic Production*, Gamble-Hinged Music Company, 1939.

WATKINS, W. J. "Producing a School Operetta", *Music Educators Journal*, Vol. XXIV, No. 1, (Sept., 1937), p. 43.

THE MARCHING BAND

DVORAK, R. F. *The Band on Parade*, Carl Fischer, Inc., 1937.

HINDSLEY, M. "The Marching Band", *Music Educators Journal*, Vol. XVII, No. 2, (Dec., 1930).

HINDSLEY, M. *Band Attention*, Gamble-Hinged Music Company, 1932.

PRE-HIGH SCHOOL MUSIC

See the first two references under Assembly Programs.

CUNDIFF and DYKEMA. *The New School Music Handbook*, C. C. Birchard & Company, 1939.

GEHRKENS, K. W. *Music in the Grade Schools*, C. C. Birchard & Company, 1934.

HUBBARD, G. E. *Music Teaching in the Elementary Grades*, American Book Company. 1934.

TRAINING THE STUDENT CONDUCTOR

MORRISON, D. *Morrison Basic Conducting Charts*, D. Morrison, Oberlin, Ohio, 1939.

OTTERSTEIN, A. W. *The Baton in Motion*, Carl Fischer, Inc., 1940.

CHAPTER TWELVE

CREATING INTEREST IN MUSIC

Music is generally an elective subject above the eighth grade. Instrumental work at all school levels must, of necessity, be on an elective basis. The conductor is, therefore, confronted with the problem of arousing interest in music if he is to have anything to conduct. This state of affairs often causes a great deal of concern among music teachers but it has some compensating features. Teaching is most enjoyable when you are working with students who are interested in their work. Very few teachers on the high school level work under such ideal conditions. The music teacher is one of those few because it is rare that anyone elects music who has no interest in the subject. There is one drawback, however, in the fact that when a subject is an elective it is often not considered to be as important as the required courses and is therefore not given equal consideration in matters of scheduling and budgeting. The music teacher is, of course, expected to make music so interesting that students will want to participate in the various activities offered. Teachers of all elective courses must make their work interesting and valuable. The present trend in education is toward more elective subjects and fewer required subjects. The music teacher with a backlog of past experience in teaching under such conditions will be in a far better position to adjust to these modern trends than will those teachers of academic subjects who have, in some instances, made little effort to make their class work interesting enough to be a success without the requirement of attendance. The music teacher will do well to consider the elective tag placed on his courses as a challenge to his teaching ability and also as added assurance that his work will be more interesting than it would be if labeled as a required course.

The necessity for arousing interest in music among the high school student body is self-evident. Many writers have stressed the importance of arousing interest in the community as well. This may seem unusual since it is not necessary to do so for other subjects in the curriculum, with the possible exception, in some instances, of athletics. Music must be "sold" to the community because the financial support of individual members of the community is needed for the program of instrumental music. Students must buy instruments. Parents must be convinced of the importance and value of music if they are to purchase instruments. There are times when it is not possible for the Board of Education to appropriate sufficient funds to purchase needed equipment and the conductor finds it necessary to attempt to raise money in the community. Theoretic-

140

ally, the Board of Education should provide the funds necessary to carry on an adequate program of music. During times of financial stress such funds are not always available. The conductor may find himself in the predicament of doing without equipment or materials, or having to raise money for their purchase. Permission must be obtained from the superintendent to raise money in the community, and the conductor should talk over with him the means to be used. Unless this procedure is taken, unfortunate relations may arise between the conductor and the superintendent.

Here is a good rule to follow when raising money. Sell only those things which give full value for money received. If a person buys a twenty-five cent ticket for a concert and gets enjoyment from the concert, he has received a return from his money and the music department has obtained some needed funds. If a family decides to attend a movie and then buys tickets from a member of the music department rather than at the box office, they have expended the same amount of money but helped the music department at the same time. This type of cooperative endeavor results in no obligation. No one has given anything for which he will expect a favor in return. Tag days, contributions from individuals, donations from civic groups and other such money-raising schemes may be necessary at times but imply obligations which should be understood at the time. Concerts (if they are good), benefit movies, bridge parties, dances, cake sales, and other similar activities are examples of money-raising projects which give a tangible return to the purchaser and the seller.

The conductor who can rely on his Board for adequate financial support and does not, therefore, have to obligate himself or his organizations to individuals or small groups in the community will do well to count his blessings.

CREATING INTEREST AMONG THE STUDENT BODY

If students become interested in a thing they talk about it at home, and then their parents become interested and talk about it to other members of the community. The logical first step in putting over a music program, therefore, is to arouse the interest of the student body. In this connection the following suggestions are offered:

1. *Make participation in musical activities an enjoyable experience.*
If the students who do elect music find that it gives them real enjoyment, that there is work as well as play, that they are more capable today than they were last week, that the music period emphasizes personal expression of the type that brings a pleasing emotional release, that the music used is more interesting than they thought it would be, then

the matter of interest will take care of itself. If on the other hand the work is so organized that the emotional element is subsidiary to the intellectual elements, the technic of music, or on the other hand, that the intellectual elements have been eliminated to the extent that there is no growth in individual power of mastery, then it may be difficult to sustain initial interests.

2.) *Organize a series of projects which will motivate the work.*

Performing groups like to work towards some specific objective. Participation is enjoyable but the knowledge that there is a definite event to look forward to will create additional enthusiasm. Public appearances make very stimulating projects. This may take the form of a full length concert, an assembly program, or a short appearance before some other body of listeners.

The operetta has proved to be one of the best projects for arousing interest in vocal music. There is much to be said for and against the operetta but as an interest-arousing project it is difficult to equal, appealing as it does to the sense of showmanship, the spectacular, the spirit of adventure, the love motive and hero worship so strong in adolescent youth.

The minstrel also combines music and showmanship and is quite popular with the boys. This type of project not only will create great interest among the student body but in the community as well. In the initial stages of building a music department it may be necessary to produce some operettas or possibly a minstrel show, which emphasize entertainment values, but as the department develops there will be a gradual transition towards more worthwhile projects which are not only entertaining but have lasting values as well. As musical taste develops it should result in a higher standard of performance of good music. Since the aims of music education will be achieved largely through development of a discriminating appreciation of music, it is essential that a department should develop projects to bring about such appreciation. Operettas may justify themselves musically only if great care is taken to select those with real musical merit.

3.)*Make music a vital thing in the life of the school.*

It should not be necessary to go to the music room in order to come in contact with music. The student body should be made conscious of music by coming in contact with it in many of the school activities. The school band should provide music at athletic contests. The orchestra should provide music for plays and similar projects sponsored by other departments of the school.

There should be some type of musical activity in most of the assembly periods. Here is a marvelous opportunity for the good assembly song leader to prove to the entire student body how enjoyable singing can be. He should compose or arrange school songs and teach them to the student body and see that they are sung at every opportunity, be it on the football field, the basketball court, the various banquets, or at commencement. He should select other infectious songs which have proved to be excellent for breaking down reserve and creating real enthusiasm. Motion songs such as *Alouette* or *Under the Spreading Chestnut Tree* have been used for this purpose with excellent results— if the conductor, himself, can forget his self-consciousness and enter into the spirit of play. Music in the assembly should not be limited to a set routine which calls for the singing of a hymn or *The Star-Spangled Banner*. Assembly participation by singing is excellent for producing interest but also music performed by special groups or individuals, or by the conductor himself for the student body, will create enjoyment and engender a desire to participate in music more extensively.

Bulletin boards should be used in the music room and the halls to display pictures and articles about musical activities, including not only those of local significance but also radio concerts and items of national importance.

The school librarian will be glad to buy a few books about music which should be of interest to students and also to arrange various displays pointing out the significance of music. Instruments may be displayed in the library with safety. If the music department is contemplating the purchase of band uniforms or choir robes, samples in school colors can be displayed in the library and the students asked to vote on their choice. In this manner, interest may be created and the students made to feel that the musical organizations belong to the student body and deserve their support.

When there is a school paper it should be used to keep the student body informed on future activities and plans. Special articles on music, particularly those which emphasize the possibility of participation in musical activities for a great majority of the student body can be used to advantage. The idea which has grown up through a period of years that only the select, talented few can play or sing needs to be discredited in every way possible.

The use of music in various classrooms should be encouraged. The music teacher should make phonograph records available to other teachers, and should be prepared to point out reference material which can be used for correlation. The language departments will generally be searching for songs to be sung in the language being studied or music written by composers of various nationalities. English literature and Art courses provide excellent vehicles for correlation with music. Certain epochs in history have been commemorated in music. Teachers of these subjects will always be happy to have material which they can use. The music teacher may, at times, be willing to visit classrooms to give short talks or demonstrations.

4. *Make the music room an attractive room which pupils like to visit.* The music room, housing as it does aesthetic experiences which appeal to the ear, should also appeal to visual sensibilities. It should provide a restful relief from the usual bare and unattractive classroom.

Whenever possible, the teacher who enjoys contacts with pupils should encourage pupil visits after school hours. The habit of dropping in the music room at the close of school to hear a recording or to visit with the teacher is a good one. Those who are not in any musical organization should be made to feel perfectly free to drop in and use the phonograph record collection. Musical enjoyment in any form and at any time should be encouraged. Those schools which can afford to support a phonograph record lending library are indeed fortunate. The time may come when most of our school and public libraries will have record collections comparable to present collections of books and will provide listening booths stocked with good reproducing instruments.

5. *The instrumental program should be started in the upper grades of the elementary school.* Players from the high school can help in arousing interest in these grades by playing for them during their assembly period. Pictures of players, instruments, and organizations can be placed in the classrooms. At least once a term each child in the elementary school should be given the opportunity of trying to play a note or two on some instrument of his choice. The use of music-talent tests of various kinds to aid in arousing interest is growing. These tests are supposed to give the parents an objective rating of their child's musical ability and to convince them that the child has enough ability to warrant purchasing an instrument for him. They should never be used for negative purposes—that is, to discourage a child's participation in music, but they may be used to discover latent talent and to encourage children to begin the individual study of music.

CREATING INTEREST IN THE COMMUNITY

The conductor at work in the schools is an educator. His first duty is to educate children. This is a large enough responsibility to keep anyone occupied and any duties assumed should be related directly or indirectly to the job of being an educator of the children in the community schools. There will be times when the educational opportunities of the students in music are being so curtailed by lack of funds that the teacher will assume a responsibility belonging to the Board of Education, that of raising funds. A great deal of thought should be given the matter and a thorough discussion of the problem held with a legal representative of the Board before this step is taken.

There are a great many ways of centering public attention on music and, specifically, the work of the local music department.

1. *Interest the student body in music.* The first and by far the most effective way of creating interest in the community is to create interest among the student body. It has been suggested previously that this method is the most satisfactory since it involves the cooperative endeavors of the parents and the students, and allows the conductor to center all of his attention where it belongs—on teaching. This approach takes for granted that the specific aim is the creation of interest in music—not the "selling" of the conductor as an indispensable member of the school faculty.

2. *Public performance by the conductor creates community interest.* The conductor who is a good performer may make some public appearances. It is well to caution the reader at this point that if one engagement is accepted, others will probably be forthcoming and may have to be accepted. It is impossible to appear before one church or club in a small community and then turn down another. Such an act would defeat its own purpose. However, public performance of superior quality by the teacher is an excellent way to gain support from the community for the music program.

3. *Student soloists should perform for community functions.* The school organizations will usually contain several soloists who need experience before an audience. Civic groups can be sent a list of the available soloists or ensembles with the suggestions that they contact the person or persons they wish to hear. This procedure will relieve the conductor of such responsibilities.

4. *Demonstrations and lectures create community interest.* The conductor should always be glad to appear before clubs or civic groups to explain the work being done in music in the schools and at that time can outline what is needed in order to make the department function successfully. This is part of his job and should not be avoided. The more persons who understand just what is being done, the easier it will be to get support when it is needed. Talks of this nature can often be arranged through school officials who are connected with civic groups. They constitute one of the most legitimate and effective means of obtaining community understanding and interest.

5. *School concerts of superior quality are indispensable.* The appearance of the band, orchestra, or choral group before the public is another excellent way of creating interest. Free public concerts show the work being done and provide entertainment at the same time. It is dangerous

to accept invitations to appear at small civic gatherings since this will make it necessary to appear at all others, but when the endeavor strictly concerns the entire community it is right and wise to have a school music group participate. Such occasions as the Memorial Day parade, the opening of the Community Chest drive, or the annual money-raising performance of the Welfare Society deserve the enthusiastic support of all school groups. Generally speaking, performances which combine music and showmanship create the most interest in the community, since people want to be entertained and are not inclined to consider the educational significance of what they hear. For this reason the operetta and marching band are two of the best projects for arousing community interest.

6. *Articles about music create community interest.* When there is a local newspaper it should be used to keep the public informed about the activities of the music department. One or two articles will do little good. There must be a continuous supply of material such as pictures of soloists, ensembles, large groups, and the conductor, also articles on every conceivable phase of music which might be of interest. Activity is an indication of life. The community should be led to see that the music department is alive and growing.

CONCLUSION

It has been proposed throughout this book that the school music conductor should be more than a conductor of music. He should be a person of broad culture, an educator, a teacher, and a general musician as well. This chapter indicates that he should also have the quality of a salesman if he is to succeed in his chosen field. The reader may feel that we are describing some paragon of perfection. However, the above qualifications are not impossible for, indeed, many of the music conductors in the schools today are approaching them.

To be a person of broad culture implies knowing something besides just music. In fact, thorough musicianship is dependent upon being cognizant and conversant with other fields of knowledge. The school music conductor should be interested in and be able to talk about other things besides music.

To be an educator implies a knowledge and understanding of the field of education, its purposes and functions in a democratic society. The music educator will use music as a means for giving young people a richer life than they would enjoy without music. He will, first of all, be interested in the development and growth of human beings and then find means by which music can contribute to this growth.

To be a teacher implies the fact that the school music conductor must be a leader. Teaching means more than instructing; it includes guiding. Guidance implies an interest in student problems and a practical understanding of the psychological procedures necessary to help the students solve their problems.

To be a general musician implies a broad, rather than a limited or over-specialized knowledge of music. The superior violinist or singer will not necessarily be a superior school music conductor. The latter should capitalize upon his forte but, at the same time, each student is individual and different and the conductor should have skilled acquaintance with various fields of music to be able to give students the right kind of guidance in musical matters. The instrumentalist should understand choral music, in order that he can better understand the problems of the choral conductor. The choral conductor should be able to conduct an orchestra and band, not only for combined performances of choral and instrumental groups, but also to be able to understand better the difficulties confronting the instrumental conductor. If there were more conductors of this type in our schools there would be more and better cooperation between the choral and instrumental departments. Moreover, it is necessary for most conductors in our schools to conduct both choral and instrumental groups.

The salesmanship qualities which a school music conductor should possess have been discussed in this chapter. It is not really necessary to "sell" music to the school and community. People have an inate and natural interest in music. However, it is necessary to sell an organized program of music with the education that it involves to both school and community and, at times, even to the administration. If the conductor has the other qualifications discussed in this conclusion he will be far along the road in attaining his goals. If he combines them with enthusiasm, and a personal and genuine interest in music and people, his success is assured.

Problems and Procedures

1. Find places where one may get pictures for use in classroom displays. Make a collection of pictures which would make an interesting unit.

2. Make a list of topics for short talks which might be of interest to civic organizations.

3. The social science teacher desires help in a class studying the Renaissance Period. Make a list of recordings which show the spirit of this age.

4. If you had $100.00 for decorating the music room, make a list of the items you would secure and indicate the approximate price of each item.

5. What successful devices for arousing interest have you seen used?

6. Make a list of topics which might be suitable for use in the school and community newspaper.

Suggestions for Further Study

Christy, Van A. *Glee Club and Chorus,* G. Schirmer, Inc., 1940, Chap. III.

Davis, E. *More Than a Pitch-pipe,* C. C. Birchard & Company, 1941, Chap. 8.

Hindsley, M. *School Band and Orchestra Administration,* Boosey-Hawkes-Belwin, Inc., 1940, Chap. XV.

Prescott and Chidester. *Getting Results with School Bands,* Paul A. Schmitt Music Company and Carl Fischer, Inc., 1938, Chap. II.

Wilson, H. R. *Music in the High School,* Silver Burdett Company, 1941, Chap. II, XVI, XVII.

APPENDIX A

ORCHESTRAL TERMS

ENGLISH	ITALIAN	GERMAN	FRENCH
Bass clarinet	Clarone	Bass Klarinette	Clarinette basse
Bass drum	Gran Cassa	Grosse Trommel	Grosse caisse
Bassoon	Fagotto	Fagott	Basson
Bells	Campane or Campanella	Glocken	Cloches
Castanets	Castagnette	Kastagnetten	Castagnettes
'Cello	Violoncello	Violoncell	Violoncelle
Clarinet	Clarinetto	Klarinette	Clarinette
Conductor	Maestro di cappella	Kapellmeister	Chef d'orchestre
Cornet	Cornetto	Cornett	Cornet à pistons
Cymbals	Piatti or Cinelli	Becken	Cymbales
Divided	Divisi (Div.)	Getheilt	à 2
Double-bass	Contrabasso	Kontrabass	Contrebasse
Double-Bassoon	Contrafagotto	Doppelfagott	Contrebasson
Double stops	Doppia fermata	Doppelgriffe	Double-cordes
Double-tonguing	Doppio colpo di lingua	Doppelzunge	Double coup de langue
Down-bow	Arco in giù	Herunterstrich	Tire
Drummer	Timpanista	Pauker	Timbalier
Desk	Leggio	Pult	Pupitre
English horn	Corno inglese	Englisches Horn	Cor anglais
Fingerboard	Tastiera	Griff brett	Touche
Flute	Flauto	Flöte	Flûte
Full score	Partitura	Partitur	Partition
Glockenspiel	Campanetta	Stahlspiel	Carillon
Gong	Tam-tam	Tam-tam	Tam-tam
Harp	Arpa	Harfe	Harpe
Horn	Corno	Horn	Cor

149

APPENDIX A—*Continued*

ORCHESTRAL TERMS—*Continued*

English	Italian	German	French
Mouthpiece	Imboccatura	Mundstück	Embouchure
Mute	Sordino	Dämpfer	Sourdine
Oboe	Oboe	Oboe	Hautbois
Orchestra	Orchestra	Orchester	Orchestre
Piccolo	Ottavino	Kleine Flöte	Petite flûte
Rehearsal	Prova	Probe	Répétition
Roll (drum)	Rollo	Wirbel	Roulement
Saxophone	Sassophone	Saxophon	Saxophone
Side-drum	Tamburo militare	Kleine Trommel	Tambour Militaire
Slide trombone	Trombone	Posaune	Trombone
String orchestra	Orchestra a corda da arco	Streichorchester	Orchestre à cordes
Tambourine	Tamburino	Tambourin	Tambourin de provence
Timpani	Timpani	Pauken	Timbales
Tonguing	Colpo di lingua	Zungenschlag	Coup de langue
Triangle	Triangolo	Triangel	Triangle
Trombone	Trombone	Posaune	Trombone
Trumpet	Tromba	Trompete	Trompette
Tuba	Tuba Bombardone	Basstuba	Tuba or Bombardon
Up-bow	Arco in sù	Hinaufstrich	Poussé
Up-beat	Levata	Auftakt	Levé
Viola	Viola	Bratsche	Alto
Violin	Violino	Violine	Violon
Xylophone	Zilafone Sticcato	Strohfiedel	Xylophon

APPENDIX B

ITALIAN PRONUNCIATION OF LATIN

By BECKET GIBBS, MUS. D.
School of Sacred Music, Union Theological Seminary
and the Juilliard School of Music

It is generally acknowledged that every country boasts of a variety of pronunciations of the national language, especially in England, with its 52 counties, each with its own peculiarities of speech. Germany and France are similar, with the northern and southern, or high and low forms of speech. Although the Latins, as a race, have ceased to exist, their language has passed into the safe-keeping of the Roman Catholic Church. The so-called Italian pronunciation might, more appropriately and more truthfully, be called the Roman pronunciation, inasmuch as the Florentine differs from the Roman, both cities boasting of their more correct form of speech. But the seat of Ecclesiastical Government being in Rome, the following rules have been most carefully collected from the best authorities in that city, while euphony has dictated the final directions, all of which have been approved by those who ought to know.

In the following phonetic spelling **aa** indicates long English **a** as in **late**; **ee** long **e** as in **seat**, etc. Each vowel has one uniform sound, whose quality is not substantially changed by its quantity. It is the neglect of this elementary principle which produces the half-Italian, half-English pronunciation which we so often hear.

- **a** This vowel has a full, open sound, as in **father**, not only in open vowels like **amo** (**ahmo**), but also in closed ones like **nam** (**nahm**).
- **e** An exact equivalent for this vowel cannot be found in our language. The nearest we have is the **a** in **fare**, or the **e** in **met**. Careful practice soon acquires it. The flat **a** as in **fat** is to be avoided.
- **ae** and **oe** equal **aa**.
- **i** This vowel is always pronounced as **ee**.
- **o** is sounded **oh**, as in **for** (**fohr**).
- **u** is sounded **oo**. For example, **cum** is pronounced **koom** and **salutaris** is **sah-loo-tah-reez**.
- **au** is pronounced like **ou** in the English word **thou**.

Used by courtesy of Dr. Becket Gibbs.

th is always pronounced as the **t** in **Thomas.** For example, **thronum** is pronounced **troh-noom.**

z is pronounced as **dz.**

c before *i, e, ae,* and *oe* is always **ch** as in **caeli** (**chaa-lee**). At all other times it is pronounced as **k.** It is *never* pronounced as **s.** When the Latin **c** is followed by *ae, oe, i,* or *e* and preceded by another *c,* the first *c* is pronounced as *t* and the second *c* as *ch,* as in **ecce** (**aat-chaa**). Another instance is **buccellas** (**boot-chaal-lahz**).

ch is always pronounced as **k.**

g is always soft before *e, i, ae,* and *oe* as in the Latin word **genitori** and in the English word **general.**

gn is **ny**; for instance, **magnam** is pronounced **mah-nyam** and **dignum** as **dee-nyoom.**

h is always silent, except in **mihi** and **nihil.**

sc before *e, i, ae,* and *oe* is like **sh** in English. Thus, **suscepi** is pronounced **soo-shaa-pee** or even **sooz-shaa-pee.**

j is always treated as **y.** Thus, **jam** is pronounced **yahm.**

ti when preceded and followed by a vowel is equivalent to **tsee.** Thus, **laetitia** is pronounced **laa-tsee-tsee-ah** and **patientia** (**pah-tsee-aan-tsee-ah**). When preceded by a consonant and followed by *a, o,* or *u,* it has the ordinary sound of **t,** as in **Christiani,** which is pronounced **kree-stee-ah-nee.**

An excellent exercise for testing one's accuracy in pronouncing the vowel sounds is to be found in reading the vowel sounds of a Latin text, passing smoothly from one to another with what might be termed a kaleidoscopic effect. Thus may be secured the utmost color from the vowels, without which vocal music would more represent an engraving than an oil or water-color painting, which is what vocal music should exhibit. For instance "et cum spiritu tuo" (*aa oo ee* **ee** *oo* **oo** *oh*) should be practiced (all voices in unison and in monotone, with perfect equality of each vowel). Again, the well-known hymn "O salutaris hostia" (*oh* **ah** *oo* **ah** *ee* **oh** *ee ah*) should be practiced. Another is "Tantum ergo sacramentum" in this form, **ah** *oo* **aa** *oh* **ah** *ah aa oo.* This method, though tedious at first, becomes interesting, while the results attained add much beauty to choral performances.

Certain words may give some trouble. The following list is far from complete, but it contains many words that are often mispronounced. The list might be added to indefinitely but it is hoped that it will be helpful to the choirmaster who desires a correct and colorful pronunciation of the Latin.

Alleluia. The first l may be treated as a musical consonant, the tip of the tongue being raised to the back of the upper teeth, keeping it there while the l is sounded. For the second l, the tongue drops to its natural position in the lower jaw. All words with double l may be treated in the same way.

Excelsis. This should be pronounced **aag-shaal-seez.** The x is sounded as **gs** and the c like **ch.** When these come together, the x loses its s sound and is softened down to **gg** and the ch is softened to **sh.** It is better to pronounce final s as z, as in the English words **bees, seas. Deus** as **day-ooz.** The z sound gives a better finish and has been approved by Roman authorities as a more agreeable ending to such words.

Fa-ctus, san-ctus, etc. Note that the **ct** in such cases belongs to the second syllable and is not divided, as is usually heard **fahk-tooz, sahnk-tooz,** etc. Such words should be *fah*-ktooz, *sahn*-ktooz, etc. There are many words with this double consonant effect and all are similarly treated. **Sanctam** (*sahn*-ktahm); **catholicam** (kah-*toh*-lee-kahm); never forgetting that the **th** is sounded as in the English word **Thomas.**

> **Aegypto** (aa-*gee*-ptoh)
> **apparebit** (ap-pah-*raa*-beet)
> **ascendit** (ah-*shaan*-deet)
> **buccellas** (boot-*chaal*-lahz)
> **descendit** (daa-*shaan*-deet)
> **dixit** (*dee*-gseet). The x belongs to the second syllable.
> **ecce** (*aat*-chaa)
> **et filio** (ate *fee*-lee-oh)
> **et spiritu** (ate spee-*ree*-too)
> **excita** (aag-*shee*-tah)
> **exquisita** (aags-quee-*see*-tah)
> **gloria** (*gloh*-re-ah)
> **inimici** (ee-nee-*mee*-chee)
> **patri** (*pah*-tree)
> **propterea** (proh-*ptaa*-raa-ah)
> **radix** (rah-*deegs*)
> **sancto** (*sahn*-cto)
> **tui** (*too*-ee)

APPENDIX C

PROGRAMS

The problem of program building is one to which all school music conductors should give major consideration. Some of the difficulties associated with this problem were discussed in Chapter Nine. One of the best ways to gain a knowledge of program building is to study successful programs. In this appendix several programs are included as examples of program building. They illustrate types of programs which have proved successful in school situations. Even more important to the reader may be the suggestions which he receives for suitable material.

The Program

Procession of Nobles . . . . *Rimsky-Korsakov*
  from the opera-ballet Mlada

Jesu, Joy of Man's Desiring . . . . *Bach*
  from Cantata 147

The Three Solitaires - Cornet Trio . . . . . . *Herbert*
  ANGELO MANSO - PHILIP RICE - HAROLD CLIFTON

Ballet Music from Faust . . . . *Gounod*

The Barber of Seville Overture . . . . *Rossini*

INTERMISSION

March - Michigan on Parade . . . . *King*

Zingaresca - Gypsy Caprice . . . . *Curzon*
  Clarinet Solo by JOHN SMITH

Birth of Dawn - Cornet Solo . . . . *Clarke*
  ANGELO MANSO

March - Americans, We . . . . *Fillmore*

Pop! Goes the Weasel and variations . Arranged by *Caillet*

March - The Desert Patrol . . . . *King*

March - The Thunderer . . . . *Sousa*

PROGRAM 1

The first program presented here was given as the eighth annual spring concert by the Port Washington High School Band of Port Washington, Long Island, Paul Van Bodegraven, Conductor. It shows the kind of music

154

possible for a good high school band to play, a band developed in a high
school of approximately 500 students. It arranges for the more serious
music to be played during the first half, and for lighter music to be played
after the intermission.

PROGRAM

PART 1.

Overture to Egmont Op. 84 . . . . Beethoven

"From the Western World", Sinfonietta . . . . . Dvorak
    I.   Allegro Risoluto
    III. Scherzo—Moltovivace

"Ballet Egyptien" . . . . Luigini
    I.   Allegro non troppo
    II. Allegretto
    III. Andante sostennto
    IV. Andante—Allegro

PART 2.

Demonstration of Instruments, and Discussion of their uses.

Four Short Pieces . . . . Bach
    I.   Chorale
    II. Minuet
    III. Sarabande
    IV. March

"Rhumba" from Second Symphony . . . . . . McDonald

PROGRAM 2

Program 2 is one which was given by the Springfield High School Orchestra, Springfield, Missouri, James Robertson, Conductor. Like the preceding program, it is divided into two parts. The unusual feature of this program is the instrumental demonstration which may be most entertaining and educational to a local audience.

PROGRAM 3

A program by the Cleveland Heights High School Symphony Orchestra, Ralph E. Rush, Conductor, is shown in number three. It illustrates the kind of music which should be played by orchestras in large high schools where music has been adequately developed. The playing of concertos to give talented students an opportunity to appear in public should be encouraged.

PROGRAM

Weber . . . . .Overture to the Opera "Oberon"

Corelli . . . . .Concerto Grosso No. 8, in G minor, Op. 6
"Fatto per la Notte di Natale"
Soloists: Violins, Elaine Sutin and Betty Spero
Cello, Rachel Protheroe; Cembalo, Phyllis Petro

Schumann . . . . . . .Concerto for Piano and Orchestra in A minor, Op. 54
I. Allegro affettuoso
Margaret Denison

Beethoven .Symphony No. 1 in C major, Op. 21
I. Adagio molto: Allegro con brio

Intermission—Ten Minutes

Bizet . . . . .Excerpts from "L'Arlesienne" Suite No. 2
Farandole
Menuetto
Soloists: Flute, Nancy Mae Iden; Bassoon, Lavern Glickman;
Harp, Marilyn Costello

Schostakowitsch . . . . .Polka from the Ballet "The Golden Age", Op. 22

Mendelssohn . . . . .Concerto for Violin and Orchestra, Op. 64
I. Allegro molto appassionato
Elaine Sutin

Borodin . . . . .Polovetsian Dances from "Prince Igor"

Program 3 includes music from the classic, romantic, and modern periods. It is a miscellaneous program which sustains its interest through variety and the general worth of the music.

PART I

CHORUS

Directed by Herbert T. Norris
Frances Miller, Accompanist

Golden Sun Streaming	Bach
Send Out Thy Light	Gounod
Now Sleeps the Crimson Petal	Quilter
Avenging and Bright	Irish Folk Song
The Cherubic Hymn	Gretchaninoff
Oh, Peddler, Tell Me	Russian Folk Song
My Bonnie Lass She Smileth	Bottomley
O Loving Saviour Slain For Us	Auber

PART II

BAND

Harold P. Wheeler, Conductor

If Thou Be Near	Bach
Overture "Youth Triumphant"	Hadley
Melody of Peace	Martin
In the Mystic Land of Egypt	Ketelbey
Fiesta-Paso Roble	Caneva-McAllister
Excerpts from "The Rose of Algeria"	Herbert
March "Pathfinder of Panama"	Sousa

PROGRAM 4

Number 4 is a concert program of the All-State High School Chorus and Band at the State College of Washington. Herbert T. Norris conducted the chorus and Harold P. Wheeler, the band. The program is a miscellaneous type from which the reader may receive ideas for materials.

PROGRAM 5

Program 5 is that of a Christmas Concert of the Clifford J. Scott High School, Orange, New Jersey. Paul L. Young was the conductor. The program was printed with the Christmas colors, green paper and red lettering. More high schools should attempt the performance of *The Messiah* and other oratorios. If any numbers were needed after the selections from *The Messiah,* the director was wise to choose familiar Christmas carols.

CHRISTMAS CONCERT

Program

Pastoral Symphony	Handel

Organ

Hark the Herald Angels Sing	Mendelssohn

Procession — — The Glee Clubs

Break Forth, O Beauteous, Heavenly Light	Bach

The Glee Clubs

------ ------ ------ ------

Selections from The Messiah by Handel

Chorus		And the Glory of the Lord
Chorus		O Thou That Tellest Good Tidings to Zion
Chorus		For unto Us a Child Is Born
Recitative	Soprano	There Were Shepherds Abiding in the Fields
		And Lo the Angel of the Lord Came upon Them
		And the Angel Said unto Them
		And Suddenly There Was with the Angel
Chorus		Glory to God
Recitative	Alto	Then Shall the Eyes of the Blind Be Opened
Air	Unison Alto Group	He Shall Feed His Flock Like a Shepherd
Air	Unison Soprano Group	Come unto Me
Chorus		Behold the Lamb of God
Chorus		All We Like Sheep
Chorus		Hallelujah

------ ------ ------ ------

Air for the G String	Bach

Modern Dance Group

Christmas Hymn	Vaughan Williams

The Glee Clubs

Two Christmas Carols from the Appalachian Mountains	collected by John Niles
1. Jesus, the Christ, Is Born	Arr. by Warrell
2. See Jesus, the Savior	Arr. by Niles
The Twelve Days of Christmas	Traditional Old English
The First Noel	Traditional
Holy Night	Adam
Silent Night	Gruber

The Glee Clubs

You will assist the performers if you will refrain from applause

PROGRAM 5
(See page
156)

PROGRAM 6
(See page 160)

—— PROGRAM ——

Part I: HEMPSTEAD HIGH SCHOOL SYMPHONY ORCHESTRA

Overture to the Opera "Oberon"   CARL MARIA VON WEBER (1786-1826)

When the three-act opera Oberon was presented to an expectant world for the first time (in London, 1826), its composer had less than two months to live. With his passing, music lost one of its most colorful personalities and influential creators. At the time the opera was produced, Weber had already experienced great success and Oberon exhibited many of the features that made the composer the "founder" of the German romantic opera. The play introduced a curious mixture of characters, among them the king and queen of Fairy-land, a knight from Bordeaux and a maiden from Bagdad. From the opening, the overture is imaginatively evocative of Fairyland and its delicate atmosphere and a splendid example of anticipatory dramatic prologue is unfolded in the work.

The overture begins with a lovely introduction, when the horn of Oberon is answered by muted strings, and delicate staccato phrases in woodwinds. After a quiet little march figure in brasses, followed by a dreamy passage in strings, a crashing chord is heard and the main body of the overture begins. After the brilliant opening measures, the horn of Oberon is again heard, answered by a skipping fairy figure. The second theme is first heard in solo clarinet and given again as conclusion to the first part, in violins. The free fantasia begins with soft repeated chords in bassoons, horns and basses, then the first theme is heard again in short phrases and a new theme is introduced against a running contrapuntal countertheme in strings. After another hearing of the second theme, the overture is brought to a spirited close.

Symphony No. 7 in A Major   LUDWIG VAN BEETHOVEN (1770-1827)

Allegretto

The Seventh Symphony has been called by many authorities one of the fullest and richest expressions of Beethoven's genius. The composer himself, in spite of increasing deafness, conducted the first performance of the great work, from manuscript, at the University of Vienna, in 1813.

The superbly beautiful second movement is fraught with special dramatic intensity and melodic appeal. The movement is really a theme and variations. The suggestion of a funeral march is powerfully present yet, after hearing it, you feel the movement is serious rather than sad and as philosophical rather than pessimistic. The music is deeply moving and communicates individually with each listener.

The first theme, in minor mode, is ominous but the second theme offers a brightening touch of hope. The rhythms of these themes, one persistent and strongly marked and the other fluent and flexible, are strangely contradictory and yet fit together as perfectly and wonderfully as some lovely mosaic. There are significant contrasts in color, tonality and rhythm, which constantly arrest the attention of the listener and cause him to again wonder at the power of the great Beethoven.

Symphonie Espagnole for Violin and Orchestra   EDOUARD LALO (1823-1892)

Alfred Breuning, Soloist

This concerto was first performed in Paris in 1875, with the great Sarsate as soloist. It had a magnificent reception and since that day has been a favorite with concert violinists, requiring virtuosity for satisfactory performance.

Allegro non troppo

The vigorous theme which opens the movement reveals the characteristic Spanish national feeling, with its alternating triple and duple rhythms. The expressive solo melody is soon heard, its flowing lines occasionally interrupted by forceful, striding steps. After a powerful orchestral phrase insisting on the alternating rhythms, the solo instrument takes up a lovely melody which leads to the tender and gracious second theme. The development offers rapid flying solo figures with chromatic chords, lending a sense of dramatic energy. A simple statement of the second subject is heard in solo violin, with lovely arabesques in the woodwind. The movement closes with a brilliant coda founded on the first theme.

Andante

The slow movement opens with a majestic theme and as the orchestral violins join the solo, the grand mood is suggestive of Beethoven. After a brief climax, a melancholy phrase on the flute introduces a finely conceived melody on the solo instrument, offering a final solo cadence which is soon evident in the other parts. The soloist soon ascends through the upper octaves to a brief cadenza, supported by peculiar knocking rhythms in the cellos. A repetition of the opening violin theme heralds the end of the slow movement, thoroughly peaceful in mood, as the solo instrument soars to ecstatic heights.

Rondo

Four measures of chords in the woodwinds set the tempo of the racy tarantella rhythm, which comes tripping from the bassoons. One by one the other instruments join the merry dance until the whole orchestra is beating the lilting time. As this music subsides, the solo violin sings a melody with agile, skipping intervals and fine, florid passages alternate with great, striding steps over a new theme in orchestral violins. The duple and triple rhythms are again repeated by the solo instrument with scintillating flourishes. The tempo gradually retards and the principal violin sings appassionato, another theme above a string accompaniment. After an extended treatment of this theme, the first violins may be heard creeping in with the opening rhythm while the flute plays the second theme. The delightfully playful movement closes with a coda which offers the soloist opportunity for fine technical display.

* * * * *

Part II: HEMPSTEAD HIGH SCHOOL A CAPPELLA CHOIR

Adoramus Te   GIOVANNI PALESTRINA (1526-1594)

This exquisite motet for four part mixed voices is attributed to the great Palestrina. The number, sung in Latin, has been adapted from the Scriptures and edited by the late Frank Damrosch, of Juilliard School of Music.

"We adore Thee, O Savior, and we do bless Thy name Jesus;
Who by Thy holy crucifixion hast redeemed Thy people.
Who for our sins hast suffered, Lord, our God,
O, Lord our God! Hearken to Thy people!"

Nightfall in Skye   HUGH S. ROBERTON

    This lovely song without words suggests a typical Skye scene at nightfall. The Scottish hills, softened by shadows, are capped by trailing mists. A white film of dew is suspended over the lily loch. Silhouetted against the sky, a woman drives her cow homeward. Humming throughout the number, the voices represent muted strings.

O, Holy Lord   NATHANIEL DETT

    This moving eight-part chorus is written by the gifted Negro composer, Nathaniel Dett. The entire composition is built about the text — "O Holy Lord! Done with Sin and Sorrow". The style is sustained and flowing and the harmonies rich and unique. Written in the style of a spiritual, the number is deeply charged with yearning and religious emotion.

The Lord Bless You and Keep You   PETER C. LUTKIN

    This beautiful benediction with Sevenfold Amen was written by the late Peter C. Lutkin, of Northwestern University.

    "The Lord bless you and keep you, The Lord lift His countenance upon you, And give you peace.

    The Lord make His face to shine upon you and be gracious unto you. Amen."

Part III: HEMPSTEAD HIGH SCHOOL SYMPHONIC BAND

On The Trail, from The "Grand Canyon Suite"   FERDE GROFÉ
Scored for Band by Eric Leidzen

    The third movement of the Grand Canyon Suite envisions a cow-boy astride his horse, guiding a pack-train of mountain burros through a Grand Canyon trail. The brays of the burros, their lazy gait, the typical song of the cow-boy, the clatter of hoofs and the rhythmic monotony of the little train are unmistakable in their clarity and significance. The lilting lift of the theme gives us a picturesque and haunting strain. The motif of the movement is simple yet the picture is clearly depicted as we hear the cowboy sing, spurring his horse in lazy fashion. The burros occasionally bray as they plod along and we may even catch an answering call from other untamed burros in the wilds. As the train nears home, it is amusing to note the characteristic pick-up in speed of the procession.

Symphony No. 1 in C Minor   ERNEST S. WILLIAMS
Ernest S. Williams, Eminent Conductor-Composer, Guest Conductor
Second Movement: Larghetto

    Although not classified as "Program Music," the inspiration of this beautiful Symphony for Band centers around the heroic life and death of Joan of Arc. The Larghetto movement discloses Joan as a prisoner, persecuted by countrymen and foreigners alike. Being alone, she needs rely upon her own unfailing faith and her anguish is somewhat soothed by memories of her former days.

    The firm faith of Joan of Arc is represented in the movement by the principal theme. The bird-like calls later heard in flute and oboe signify childhood memories. The winding, descending theme, sombre and sinuous in character, symbolize her accusers, while the jagged and rough theme typifies the violence she encounters from the infuriated mob. In closing the movement, we leave the heroine in religious meditations.

Concertino for Clarinet and Band   CARL MARIA VON WEBER
Arr. M. L. Lake

    Arthur Christman, Metropolitan Opera Symphony, as Soloist

    The blithe and colorful music of the Weber Concertino for Clarinet makes it one of the most popular solos for the instrument. It displays the pure beauty of tone color of the clarinet in its different registers and offers the performer ample opportunity for fine technical display. Although not heavily scored for band, the arrangement offers a setting of beautiful tonal contrasts, impressive in volume and sonority and accurate in balance between soloist and band.

    The first part of the composition is a theme and variations. After a lengthy introduction marked Adagio, in which the solo instrument is heard against a rich woodwind background, the main theme is heard,— a lovely song-like andante. After a spirited interlude for both solo and band, the solo instrument offers its first variation on the main theme, featuring lovely designs in triplet figures. Variation II follows, embellishing the theme with more elaborate sixteenth-note passages.

    In contrast, we next hear a quiet Lento section, in which the rich, low tones of the solo instrument are heard against a woodwind setting. The final section is a spirited Allegretto, in which the solo part appears in brilliant technical passages, gay and fantastic in style, while the band setting provides pleasant instrumental contrast.

Bolero   MAURICE RAVEL (1875-1937)
arr. by Mayhew Lake

    This famous Bolero was dedicated to a Parisian dancer who first presented the work in Paris in 1928. The staging suggested a Spanish Inn, the dancer appearing on a table. The mounting excitement of the music, with the hypnotism of the persistent rhythms and the imagination of the dancer herself, is said to have brought about such a disorderly scene at this first performance that audience and actors alike were involved and the dancer barely escaped injury. The Bolero was first performed in America at Carnegie Hall in New York City, by the New York Philharmonic Symphony, under Toscanini, in 1929.

    In the opening of the number, drums give out the dance rhythm which is persistently maintained throughout the work. The oboe first announces the main theme, which is in turn sung by the clarinets. The same theme, each time in the same rhythmical setting, is next sung by solo bassoon and is again heard in solo flute. Finally, the full instrumentation of the band attacks the theme. We feel the suspense of the gradual crescendo from the beginning until an explosive modulation brings about the close in a "tornado of sound."

    This has been called a clever study in instrumentation and a sound study in psychology. The use of unvarying rhythms, charged with primitive flavor, carries us beyond the point of boredom to the verge of madness. The execution of the work is original and superbly effective.

National Anthem: The Star Spangled Banner   FRANCES SCOTT KEY
Symphonic Band, A Cappella Choir, with Audience

PROGRAM 6
Continued
(See page 160)

Program 6 (pages 158-159) is of a joint concert which was given by the music organizations of Hempstead High School, Hempstead, Long Island. Imogene Boyle was conductor of the orchestra and band; Esther McQueen was conductor of the a cappella choir. The program indicates an advanced stage of music development. No time was lost in shifting the stage equipment, for the choir risers were placed in front of the stage and the stage was set for the instrumental organizations. Elaborate program notes were written for each number.

```
                               PROGRAM
        I. Orchestral Numbers

           Overture to "The Magic Flute" K.620 ... Wolfgang Amadeus Mozart


           Symphony No.5 in E Minor, Op.95 (New World) .... Antonin Dvorak
              Adagio, Allegro Molto
                 Largo
                 Scherzo


           Rapsodie Negre ................................... John Powell



       II. Choral Numbers

           Early Secular Music
              Now Start We with a Goodly Song ............. Hans Leo Hasler
              Aye Me, Alas, Hey Ho ......................... Thomas Weelkes
              Which Is the Properest Day to Sing? ............ Thomas Arne

           Sacred Music
              Motet, Op.29, No.2 ......................... Johannes Brahms
              Create in me, O God, a pure heart
              O cast me not away from Thy countenance
              Grant unto me the joy of Thy salvation

           Folk Music
              Norwegian Echo Song ..................... Arr. by R. H. Smith
              Mother, Do Not Scold Me ........ Russian - Arr. by H. Wilson
              The Quarrel ................. Ukrainian - Arr. by A. Koshetz

           Contemporary Music
              O Brother Man .............................. Harold E. Darke
              White Waves on the Water .................. Hugh S. Roberton
              Prologue ................................. William H. Schuman
```

Program 7 is one given by the summer session orchestra and chorus of Teachers College, Columbia University, Norval L. Church and Harry R. Wilson, Conductors. Program notes were supplied for the orchestral numbers, and words, for the choral. The program is too long for most school programs, which should not be over one hour and a half in length. There are suggestions for many new choral numbers.

PROGRAM

Spiritual - Fantasia   *Arr. by Holmes*
                                       BAND

Festival Prelude - from "Die Meistersinger"   *Wagner*
                       CHORUS AND ORCHESTRA

Twenty Third and Twenty Fourth Psalms
                       POETRY SPEAKING CHORUS

(a) Annie Laurie   *Arr. by Geibel*
(b) Hail Bright Abode - from "Tannhauser"   *Wagner*
                       BOYS CHORUS

(a) The Dance   *Rossini*
(b) None But The Lonely Heart   *Tschaikowsky*
                       LEO GLANTZ - VIOLINIST
(c) Sapphire Seas - from "The Firefly"   *Friml*
                       MARGARET KEMP - SOLOIST
(d) Swing Your Partner - from "Shvanda"   *Weinberger*
                       VOCAL AND INSTRUMENTAL ENSEMBLE

The Loreley   *Liszt*
Lift Thine Eyes - from "Elijah"   *Mendelssohn*
                       GIRLS CHORUS

Allegretto from "Seventh Symphony"   *Beethoven*
                       ORCHESTRA

(a) Six Love Songs   *Brahms*

      I   A tremor's in the branches - Op. 52 No. 18
      II   Nightingale, thy sweetest song - Op. 52 No. 15
      III Birds in air will stray afar - Op. 52 No. 13
      IV   From yon hills the torrent speeds - Op. 65 No. 7
      V   Locksmith, ho! a hundred padlocks! - Op. 52 No. 12
      VI   Now, ye Muses, be hushed - Op. 65 No. 14
                       MIRIAM WEISMAN - ALICE COATS
                       At the pianos

(b) Second Movement - Fifth Symphony   *Tschaikowsky*
                       CONCERT CHOIR

                       Community Singing
Love's Old Sweet Song   *Malloy*
Old Folks At Home   *Foster*
                       LED BY MR. SMITH

Cantata "The Swan and Skylark"   *Thomas*
                       CONDUCTED BY MR. KOLAR

(a) The Lost Chord   *Sullivan*
(b) Gettysburg Address   *Hadley*
(c) Democracy Forever   *Gaines*
                       CHORUS AND ORCHESTRA

PROGRAM 8

The program of the annual music festival of Central High School,
Detroit, Michigan, is No. 8. It presents a resume of the year's work,
including numbers by the band, orchestra, chorus, boys' chorus, girls'
chorus, poetry speaking chorus, combined ensemble, and soloists. The
program was under the direction of Harry Seitz. Victor Kolar, Director
of the Detroit Symphony Orchestra, was guest conductor. The program
includes community singing led by Fowler Smith. Care must be taken in
presenting programs of this nature that there is not too much delay in
stage shifting, and that the program does not become too long.

PROGRAM 9 (See page 162)

Program 9 is that of the concert of the eighth annual music festival
of the Lake Erie League, a group of high schools in the vicinity of Cleveland. The program builders very wisely interrupted the procession of
a cappella choirs with a number by string orchestra. Festivals of this
nature are fine activities to organize in any section. Choir members have
a chance to hear each other, and conductors can compare their work and
get new ideas. The program is rich in choral material.

Program

LAKEWOOD A CAPPELLA CHOIR

On the Morrow..............................Samuel Richard Gaines
Drink to Me Only With Thine Eyes.................Johnson-Blakeslee
The Long Day Closes..............................Arthur Sullivan
Spirit ob de Lord Done Fell......................Noble Cain

DIRECTED BY THELBERT EVANS

ELYRIA A CAPPELLA CHOIR

The Cherubic Hymn.........................Alexander Gretchaninof
Lost in the Night............................F. Melius Christiansen
In the Night Christ Came Walking.................Noble Cain
I Won't Kiss Katy (Yugo--Slav Folk Song)..Smith-Aschenbrenner
Angelus ....H. Clark

DIRECTED BY J. MARTIN BECK

SHAKER A CAPPELLA CHOIR

Salvation is Created..............................A. Tschesnekof
Judge Me, O God.................................Carl Mueller
Sometimes I Feel Like a Motherless Child..........Arthur Ward
Three Love Songs.............................Johannes Brahms
   A Tremor's in the Branches
   Nightingale Thy Sweetest Song
   From Yon Hills the Torrent Speeds

DIRECTED BY REYNOLD ELLIS

FESTIVAL STRING ORCHESTRA

(String Quartets from Lakewood, Lorain and Cleveland Heights)
Fantasia-Symphonette, based on familiar melodies by
Mozart and Brahms

DIRECTED BY RALPH E. RUSH

LORAIN A CAPPELLA CHOIR

Cherubim Song.................................Michael Glinka
God's Mercy...................................Griffith J. Jones
Deep Purple...................................Peter deRose
The Donkey Serenade from "The Firefly"..Friml-Stothart-Warnick

DIRECTED BY S. NORMAN PARK

Program

CLEVELAND HEIGHTS A CAPPELLA CHOIR

Tenebrae in Eb.........................Michael Haydn-Strickling
Star Dust.......................Carmichael-Webster-Strickling
Tradi Nuka (Latvian Frolic)......................Austris Wihtol
Beautiful Saviour.........................F. Melius Christiansen

DIRECTED BY GEORGE F. STRICKLING

SHAW A CAPPELLA CHOIR

How Lovely are Thy Messengers from "St. Paul"..................
   ....Felix Mendelssohn
My Johnny Was a Shoemaker (Cornwall Air).........Deems Taylor
Dusk ....Alexander Gretchaninof
A Violin Is Singing in the Street (Ukrainian Song)..............
   ....Alexander Koshetz

DIRECTED BY MISS FLORENCE SHAFFER

COMBINED CHORUS

Men and Angels Sing Alleluia.................J. and T. Edwards-Jones

DIRECTED BY J. MARTIN BECK

I Hear You Calling Me.................Charles Marshall-Howorth
Ave Maria......................Franz Schubert-Strickling
   Violinists from the Festival String Orchestra
   Harpist—Marilyn Costello

DIRECTED BY GEORGE F. STRICKLING

Old Ark's a-Moverin' (Spiritual)................Noble Cain

DIRECTED BY J. MARTIN BECK

PROGRAM 9 (See page 161)

SPRING FESTIVAL OF SONG

Opera Choruses
Sung by Choral Society and selected group
from Opera Club

I. TWO CHORUSES FROM "ORPHEUS"   Gluck

   "If here, where all is dark"
   "From the realm of souls departed"

II. LAMENT (SOLO) AND FINAL CHORUS
   FROM "DIDO AND AENEAS"   Purcell

   "When I am laid in earth"
   "With drooping wings ye cupids, come"

III. CHORUS FROM "ROSAMUNDE"   Schubert

   "Forth to the meadows"

IV. CORONATION SCENE FROM
   "BORIS GODUNOW"   Moussorgsky

High School Opera Club

OPERA AIRS

   "Devotion" arranged from "Cavelleria Rusticana"
                           Mascagni
   "Hail, All Hail" arranged from "Carmen"   Bizet
   "Triumphal March" from "Aida"   Verdi

INTERMISSION

V. CHORALE AND FINALE
   FROM "DIE MEISTERSINGER"   Wagner

   "Awake! draws nigh the break of day"
   "Honor your native masters"

VI. AIRS AND CHORUSES
   FROM "LA BELLE HELENE"   Offenbach

   1. "Voici les Rois de la Grece"
   2. "Je suis le bouillant Achille"
   3. "On me nomme "Helene la blonde"
   4. "Le voici le Roi des Rois"
   5. "Partez, noble Reine"

Greenwich Academy Chorus

TEN GERMAN DANCES   Schubert

   1. "Ring out ye voices, resounding in song"
   2. "On forest verge how sweet is rest"
   3. "Come, darling, in the dance let us gyrate now"
   4. "As the suff'rer longs for day-dawn's glowing"
   5. "Wait a while, boy so impatient"
   6. "When love-fraught sighs come softly cooing"
   7. "To doubt and to dread an end shall be made"
   8. "High beat the heart's pulses"
   9. "As dew-drops lie gleaming on petals of rose"
   10. "Hark! merry bells chiming"

VII. AIRS AND CHORUSES
   FROM "THE BARTERED BRIDE"   Smetana

   1. "Why not sing of joy and gladness"
   2. "Join my swaying, turning, swaying"
   3. "What's your decision, come tell us, Marie"
   4. "A clever lad, too smart for me"
   5. "Rich success our task enlightens"

   Combined Choruses

PROGRAM 10

As a worthy example of a community concert illustrating how school
organizations may combine with community groups Program 10 is offered.
It is a program of a choral concert by the Greenwich Choral Society,
Greenwich Academy Chorus, and Greenwich High School Opera Club, all
of Greenwich, Connecticut. Lowell P. Beveridge and Mary C. Donovan
were the conductors. It emphasizes the singing of choruses from the
operas, a field of music literature which is often neglected in our schools.

Eleventh Annual Spring Concert

Trenton State Teachers College Choir

Kendall Hall, Hillwood Lakes

Program

Hodie Christus Natus Est	*Healey Willan*
Today Christ is Born	
Oh, Praise Ye	*Tschaikowsky*
Serenade	*Arensky*
('Cello Obbligato, George Barati)	

Will O' The Wisp	*Charles Gilbert Spross*
The Evening Star	*Granville Bantock*
My Johann	*Edward Grieg*
Women's Chorus	
Dorothy Ziegler, Accompanist	

From Grief To Glory, A Suite . . .	*F. Melius Christiansen*
Three Movements	
Decadence	
Love in Grief	
Spring Returns	
The Choir	

Now Sleeps The Crimson Petal . . .	*M. Andrews*
Joshua Fit The Battle, Negro Spiritual . .	arr. *Harvey Gaul*
Men's Chorus	
Alan Langford, Accompanist	

Roll Chariot	*N. Cain*
Cuckoo Song	*L. Lemlin*
Longing For Home	*Kjerulf*

Carol M. Pitts, Director

PROGRAM 11

This is an example of a
choral program featuring
the Trenton State Teachers
College Choir, Trenton,
New Jersey, assisted by the
Women's Chorus and the
Men's Chorus, Carol M.
Pitts, Director. It provides
unusual variety.

Ye womenne will kindlie remove ye bonnets which may obstruct ye sight of others. Ye hair may be retained.

Approval of ye syngers' effortes may be expressed in seemly fashion, but loud stampynge and scrapynge of ye feet will not be allowed.

YE FIRST PARTE

1. *Olde Tyme Tunes* - - - - - - - Ye Skule Orkestra
Fortissimo Worthington Bayers, Dyrector

2. *Song of ye Olde Folke* - - - - - - - Ye Fulle Choire

3. *Rolle Calle* - - - - Ye Towne Cryer, Sonorous Beready Dean

4. *Strike ye Cymbal* - - - - - - - - - - Ye Choire

5. *My Grandma's Advice* - - - - - - - Blessed Bodine

6. *Anvil Chorus* - - - - - - - Ye Menne and Chorus

7. *Ye Keys of Heaven* - - - Joyous Symphonia Adams and
Rallentando Epaphroditus Gaffney

8. *Songs from ye "Sacred Harp"* - - Ye Facultie Hymn Syngers

9. *Three Rounds* - - - - - - - - Ye Whole Companie

10. *O Dear, What Can ye Matter Be?* Rosebud Crescendo Nicolaisen

11. *Columbia ye Gem of ye Ocean* - - - Ye Treble and Choire

12. *Reuben and Rachel* - - - - - Nepenthe Seymour and
Highsee Jehoshaphat Madden

13. *Cousin Jedediah* - Ritardando Ezekiel Whittaker and Chorus

At ye conclusion of ye First Parte, they in olde tyme costume may visit among ye assemblage while ye womenne gossip and ye menne discuss ye affaires of state.

Let young menne and maidens among ye students act not unseemly but be discreet in their manners. Virtue is its own reward. (Also ye headmaster will be present and skule is not yet over.)

Kindlie use snuff with care: ye syngers are not to be sneezed at!

Young menne are asked not to gaze too fixedly at ye maidens who may synge. They are easily distracted and may skyp a beatte.

YE SECOND PARTE

1. *Overture Bucolique* - - - - - - - Ye Same Orkestra
Tymester: Fortissimo Worthington Bayers

2. *Ye Spacious Firmament* - - - - - - Ye Greate Choire

3. *O No, John* - - - - - - - - Jezebel Francisco and
Robusto Jerusalem Tolmie

4. *Ye Dearest Spot of Earth* - - - Ye Womenne and Choire

5. *Allicante* - Solo on ye Clarionet by Fortissimo Worthington
Bayers, accompanied at ye piano-forte by Miss Judith Andrews

6. *General Synge* - - - - - - - - - - All ye People

7. *Chester* - - - - - - - - - - - Ye Small Choire
(A song by Wm. Billings, ye first professional composer of ye
American Colonies.)

8. *I Would That My Love* - - - Araminta Miriam Scott and
Remembrance Euterpe Hatcher

9. *Yankee Doodle* - - - - - - - Ye Menne and Chorus

10. *Ye Synging Lesson* - - - - Heavenly Rosalia Snyder and
Harmonium Longemeasure Woodruffe

11. *Hail Columbia* - - - - - - - - - All ye Syngers

12. *Auld Lang Syne* - - - - - - - Ye Entire Assemblage

Ye players of ye piano-forte are Blessed Bodine and Naomi Soundkey Clarke

On thys occasion, young menne are permitted to accompanie ye maidens and see them safely home, but in no case to linger longe at ye gayte.

PROGRAM 12

An unusual example of a novelty program is shown in Program 12.[1] It is an "Olde Folkes' Concerte" presented with many amazing and entertaining features by Ye Student Choire and Certayne Members of Ye Facultie of Ye Roger Ludlowe High Schule in Ye Village of Fairfield, Connecticut, precentor: Harmonium Long Messure Woodruffe (Harvey L. Woodruff). Even the tickets and the frontispiece of the program were printed in "Ye Olde Englishe". The singers were dressed in old-fashioned costumes, and each, along with the conductor, had appropriate names based on the initials of their first names. The program began with the singers strolling informally down the aisles to take their places on the stage. It includes a roll call of the singers. It enlists the services of the students, faculty, and audience. An occasional program of this nature can be most enjoyable.

---

[1] This program is described in detail in the article "Have You Tried An Olde Folkes' Concerte?" in the *Music Educators Journal*, September-October, 1941, Music Educators National Conference.

INDEX